REMEMBERING ONE,
ONCE AGAIN

REMEMBERING ONE,
ONCE AGAIN

TWELVE PRINCIPLES THAT
WILL CHANGE YOUR LIFE

Tammy J. Holmes

Copyright © 2012 by Tammy J. Holmes

Artwork: Ann Lee Rothan
Cover design: Crystal McMahon
Interior design: Don Enevoldsen

Library of Congress Cataloging-in-Publication Data
Holmes, Tammy J.
   Remembering one, once again : the twelve principles that will change your life/ Tammy J. Holmes. — 1st ed.
      p.cm.
ISBN 978-0-9853743-0-3 (paper)
1. Spirituality. 2. Self-actualization (Psychology) 3. Self-perception.
   I. Title.

Paper ISBN: 978-0-9853743-0-3

Library of Contress Control Number: 2012907667

1st edition, April 2012

Printed in the United States of America

 Learn more information at:

www.tammyjholmes.com

To my heart Jane Landers, for your love and support. Without your encouragement and love this book would not have been written. Thank you for coming into my life when everything fell apart. You told me it was the prefect time. I wish for everyone to have a Jane in their lives.

To my dear son James, for choosing me as your mother. You have made me a better person and held me responsible to be present with you. Even through all our cycles, we still come together, seeing the beauty in each other.

To William, my mentor and teacher, for keeping me focused and moving forward. Your stern guidance and unconditional love carried me when I could not make sense of things. You gave clarity to Our existence. Your loyalty to serve all of us inspires me to embrace the God self in me.

I Pray that as we alter our awareness to our Oneness that we no longer require pain as a form of learning, that we embrace joy and laughter as our primary frequency, and that we do not need to remember anything ever again because we are One, complete God Selves.

May your hearts be touched and your minds be transformed into realms of Oneness.

CONTENTS

INTRODUCTION TO THE TWELVE PRINCIPLES

You will be changed from the twelve principles if you follow them. I did not have a clue I would be writing this book. The book title and subheadings came to me in 2007 when I was not yet ready to come out of the pain cycle. I was deep in fear and addicted to the rush of doing things. I thought I had to keep doing more to get the results I wanted. With my heart fully engaged in outcomes, I had only moments of love—mostly fear prevailed.

I believed I had it all going on. In fact, I was just barely hanging on to what I thought would make me happy. In 2008, I was walking to the laundry room with a basket of dirty clothes when I heard a voice say, "You are not playing with a full deck." I knew this voice was coming from inside my head. I stopped quickly and put down the load of clothes. I immediately said to the voice, "How could I while I still occupy a body?" The voice then replied, "You can. Here are the twelve principles and subheadings that will show you how it can be done." The voice that was going on in my head gave me the twelve principles and subheadings in less than half an hour. I wrote down all the information as fast as I could and then had to rewrite it all because I could not read some of my writing. I was blown away to say the least. I have been doing readings and coaching for over fifteen years, and this moved me to tears. It was like nothing I had ever felt before. I knew these principles would work, but to my embarrassment, I was not yet ready to try them out on my own. I was in the middle of producing an event, and I decided to put away the principles in a folder in the file cabinet until I was ready to look at them. I allowed myself to experience more pain and suffering until I could not do it anymore. I need to acknowledge that many wonderful souls came in to help me out as much as they could. Without those wonderful beings, probably not all of the events would have happened.

The year was 2010 when I started to write about the principles, and William was eagerly waiting (with much support) for me to do this. As I was writing the book, I came to know the voice in my head as William, my brother from the 1600s, who is an ascended being from the Council of Twelve. William has moved me forward with his energy of love and passion for a better way for all of us. The patience that William has for me is also the patience William and the angels have for you.

I had to lay down my judgments about this book or I could not have written it at all. I have completely surrendered the outcome of the book, including how it needs to look. The voice is speaking through me to write, and I am compelled to do so because of a needed change within me. Maybe you will feel the need to change your own lives.

I am not perfect and I have made many turns in my life that could have been easier. Many of my choices created unnecessary pain. I became tired and confused to the point of complete surrender. That is when this book started to write itself. What I know to be true is that because of the hardships I have chosen to experience, I have been led to write this book for you, for myself, and for William, to share how we can be happier beings on this planet.

Sometimes along the way, I have not shown up as coming from love—please forgive me. I am now willing to live my life with these principles in hand, especially as they help me get past the struggle and pain I have been experiencing. With all of the Earth experiences right now and the intense desire that we all should be more productive, we need to come from love and let go of the attachments to outcomes for happiness. To be redeemable and humbled are gifts within all of us. I am now willing to go inward to a journey worth living. You have a choice to create differently. I hope you are with me.

The stories in this book are true. Many of the names have been changed. Some names have not been changed, and for those people

I was granted permission to include their story. The messages from William will lift your spirits. In the writing of the book William is like a stern teacher who is very passionate about our planet and his belief that we can change our world to be more light-filled as unified beings working together toward a common purpose. William's vision for our planet is to thrive by helping us move into the universal heavens. For me to know William is to know myself better than I ever believed possible. I give you William as a confidant and someone you can lean on anytime you desire. William is pure love. His words will ring true to your soul. You will discover the wind of hope, perseverance, and victory for your life, allowing you to show up differently once and for all, while at the same time allowing your inner wisdom to move through your thoughts, directing you into waves of joy, harmony and trust. You will have faith in yourself again, agreeing to have your God Self walking this planet.

I have been deeply blessed to have met so many incredible souls. The workshops, conferences, readings, and coaching sessions have given me so many healing experiences. All of the events I have produced and the team of angels who have shown up to believe with me have inspired me to move forward and not to be defined by my works or deeds, but by the heartfelt connections that we make along the way. Please do not wait as long as I did to begin this journey.

As you read the conversation between William and I, you will see all of my comments in italics. This will make it easier for you to follow. Also in the book I have capitalized WE, so that you will know when the ascended beings are talking. I hope you enjoy the principles. May they lift your energies to new beginnings of transformational happiness, allowing you to remember your Oneness once again through our collective agreement to co-create hope and renew our planet, enabling it to cycle back into complete Light.

With much love and joy,

Tammy J. Holmes

REMEMBERING ONE, ONCE AGAIN

The 1st Principle:
BE PEACE WITHIN

The more you cling to the struggle and pain,
the further you are from the solution.

Isn't it true that everyone you know, including yourself, would rather learn through joy and without pain? You will learn from joy or pain. It is your choice. WE do not believe for a second that anyone would knowingly choose a painful way to learn. Our soul knows no difference between good, bad, joy, or pain. The soul's requirement is to propel you into your development of a higher frequency that will allow you to discover your true essence of love, God, completeness, and Oneness.

Our work on this planet is to grow soulfully and to be inspired to live our calling, our contract, and our purpose. WE agreed before WE incarnated to remember that being One again—part of the collective as one being—is also to learn and grow. You will get it now or later—it is up to you.

You also know deep down that if you are honest with yourselves that most of you learn through pain. As you get older, most of you start to understand that the lessons can be of joy and do not have to come through painful struggles or experiences. These principles are given so that you can avoid hardship and take ownership of what is possible by following these steps to live with more joy and love in your lives.

WE, your guides, watch you trip over and over again, only to have moved not forward into a brighter place, but into a cycle that repeats until the deepest grooves are made symbolically like a broken record. Some of you have stayed in those grooves most

5

of your lives, to no avail. You stay there until a painful situation is created by you to pull yourself out. The most important thought you can make as you wallow in struggles and pain is to know that you have a choice to change it. You also need to know that you created the experience. No matter how many players have shown up to validate your pain, remember that you created the experience. How many times do you need to repeat your cycle or call in different players to play it out? It really is up to you. The results will always be the same if you are vibrating from a place of pain and struggle; you will continue to create more pain and struggle. WE are eagerly waiting for you to move out of it. Of course, WE are here with much love and compassion, because WE, like you, have lived in incarnated bodies. So let's go over what struggle and pain look like.

WE will give you all kinds of examples of what the different types of pain look like in Chapter One. You will know you have arrived in the pain and struggle cycle when you feel you have lost something, or you have no power over an occurrence that has happened to you or someone you know, when things did not happen the way you wanted, and you were attached to the outcome, expecting it to be the key to your happiness. When "it" did not happen, you then felt lost, betrayed, hurt, confused, angry. WE could go on and on, but the lowest frequency to hold is victim energy, where you feel like a victim of the act that took place. Once you are there in that energy, you will create more struggle and pain to validate your thoughts and feelings about being victimized. It is a no-win experience.

Once you are in this lower frequency, you start to believe whole-heartedly that you have been violated. You feel life is not fair. Then the stories become more powerful, and you repeat them over and over as you talk about them. You vacillate between blaming yourself and someone else or maybe even a whole group of people. You become your pain, and it shows in every way. Your energy shows it, your body shows it, and your life starts to show it. It affects your family and your community and most of your entire world. Remember that occasionally you are part of the effect of someone else's pain, which can also create the cycle of pain for you. What

WE are witnessing (and this has gone on for centuries) is the pain cycle. That is why your planet is in despair and needs to be returned to its original state of Oneness and harmony.

These principles were given to Tammy because—along with you—she has continued to repeat her struggles to learn the truth about why she knew she *had* to produce the conferences. The energy engaged her being-ness until she did the last two conferences. It came to a point where her soul wanted her to learn what she needed, even if it was through pain and struggle. Tammy finally got the lessons and learned so much.

Tammy's note: In 2009 I was guided to produce two conferences which brought in some of the highest-minded teachers on our planet. They were big-name productions, involving well-known and famous teachers from the spiritual teaching industry. Many others helped me work tirelessly on this project to share the good news with the masses. While the messages were remarkable and I learned much, the conferences were not a financial success. The lessons that I learned from the experience could fill volumes of books, but more about that in a bit. Afterwards, I felt as if I had not accomplished what I set out to accomplish; that I had sacrificed everything for the higher good and emerged a victim. I felt I was a victim of some of the teachers who did not even bother to help market the conferences. I felt like I was a victim of the economy. I felt like I was a victim of the Universe. I also take responsibility for all of my choices that were made by me, that were not in my best interest or for my business. How could this happen to me when I had only the highest of intentions? This book, in part, is the answer to those questions. William and I will discuss this in just a bit, but I want to explain how this book came about.

We do not want to give a lot of energy to all of the adjectives describing what pain looks like. We must look at some of the wavering personality traits that tend to show up as you vacillate into victim cycle. You start to doubt yourself. You doubt life and your beliefs.

You realize you do not know what the truth is anymore. All this is because you actually are in energy of fear that is confusing and altered—in energy that is not truth. You are vibrating away from truth, love, peace and the all-knowing frequency of God. No wonder you are confused!

One of the traits that WE see all too often is that once you allow yourself to be in this energy, addictions arise. Because of the frequencies of this state, many souls start to punish themselves. They drink, smoke, or eat—whatever the vice is—to feel better. Unfortunately, you will feel worse. This trap holds many grievances to the soul and can take many lifetimes to repair.

It is obvious when you are in the pain that you will pull in other players who are in the same boat. Misery does love company. If you want to be honest with yourself, look around when you are in pain and observe what happens to the people in your life who are happy; they tend to leave and not show up again until your energy vibrates with theirs again. That is a huge clue something has changed in you.

In this frequency, God is not away from you at all. You are away from God. You have pulled away from your essence. The interesting part of this is that you will stay away until it is so uncomfortable that you will finally return to the Light with vigor and hope. It is just like a stretched rubber band that snaps back into its original shape. Your essence always returns to its original source. You will return to Source in this lifetime or later. In fact, you can do this many times in only one lifetime.

The choices you make have an undercurrent of energy that touches everyone on this planet; those choices have a ripple effect that touches thousands and thousands of other souls as you move in and out of your day. What a tall order that is, and think about the difference you make to others.

How are you playing that card out? I told Tammy when I delivered the chapter titles and principles that she was not playing with a full deck. I meant that she was not dealing well in her vibration and that the effect could change for her.

At the time, Tammy was not ready yet, and she was in the midst of her despair. She is now ready and willing to move out of pain and struggle. Tammy's vibration has moved into a place where she is asking, *"What can I do now?"* Tammy is now ready to write this book, with help from me, William.

Tammy is a soul committed to the journey of truth, even at her own expense. I say no more suffering for her and anyone else who wants to learn and know the ways. These steps are a part of the spirit guides' gifts to download to everyone, so that joy again can reign in the world WE still believe in. I know as Tammy is writing this she thinks she has gone crazy, but she has gone sane and is connected. This is the beginning of our dear and heartfelt conversation between Tammy and me, William.

I am William and I am here to serve her calling to share with you what God and all of us in a higher frequency would have you know that you can believe in. Tammy was my brother in the 1600s and served well and died for a cause that was not worthy. So I am here to redeem myself to her as a brother and as a soul that is willing to change the world to a much better place.

I am one Light Being that works with many. I represent four different realms of time and space. I go between all of these realms to assist with energies.

What do you mean by that?

I work with the Council of Twelve and the Holy Spirit to direct Light where it is needed. I am a conduit for healing, giving freedom from forces that plague all of the four realms with despair.

Why only four?

Because above the four realms, it is not needed.

Why?

Because beyond the four realms is only Light and there are no forces of darkness. Your world thrives on the darkness and then begs for the Light again. It is like watching a Ping-Pong rally that never ends. You keep dropping the ball to play a game you can never win at on your own.

With the assistance of the Holy Spirit and the forces of Light, you can regain your composure to make wiser decisions for yourself. You will lay down the paddle. It is so easy to fall short or, as the Course In Miracles says, be in your wrong mind. It is extremely easy to be lost in the darkness; however, these principles should help you if you allow yourself to work them.

I am so ready.

Yes, you can beat yourself down like a rag doll until you ask for another way. Or you can just stop the play of a really endless Ping-Pong game you cannot win on your own.

I surrender to that and I bet all the readers will too.

WE pray that they do.

Who are the "WE" that you are referring to?

The Council of Twelve. WE are also the guides, ascended beings, and ascended masters.

What?

WE are all that is past, present and future, and all spirit forces that are seen and not seen that vibrate with complete love.

I understand!

Yes, you do. The Council of Twelve is twelve teachers in spirit who serve a voice of truth collectively to give guidance to all of us. Remember when you went into meditation to hear from the Council during a time when you were producing an event in 2007?

Yes I do.

Well, I was one of them and decided I wanted to help you move past your struggles. I am committed to show you that it can be done and it will be done. I also was your brother in the 1600s.

Ok I do remember the remarks that were given to me. All I heard was that I had perseverance and that was it. So I was not sure you were helping me.

WE are always helping you and everyone else on your planet. Can we get back to the chapter in hand?

Sure.

Remember, if your perceptions are not <u>aligned</u> to love and acceptance, than the first example of pain is not allowing change to be a part of your life. Your life will call in many changes in the duration of your time on earth because your soul thrives on internal shifts to learn from. The pain is a false sense of security that depends on the external play not changing, which is an illusion. The only security is within, where God lives.

When things change, change with them. Try not to struggle with changes. You all know they happen for reasons you cannot see at the time. Sometimes you know why you are going through the changes, and there is no struggle with it. But when you feel your safety or happiness lies in the external parts of your world, that becomes a mixture for much pain. Embracing the change will make it much easier.

So, Tammy, tell them about your painful experiences, especially the year 2009, and how hard that was on you.

Do I have to?

Yes you do.

Ok. I had this intense desire to put on spiritual events. It took me like a wave that knocked me to my knees in the ocean. I had mixed emotions about them. I've produced over fifteen events since 2000 and had much fear show up in every one. I was even unsure why I was doing them; however, my heart was deeply motivated to bring groups of people together to share in the love of God. The desire was to feed us all to move us to change within so we can change the world.

The events got bigger and bigger—by design. In 2009, I was guided to put together two "mega-conferences" involving multiple teachers, some of the biggest names in the spiritual teaching industry. This also meant that these were the highest paid. The price tag for these events, both in terms of monetary and energetic expenditures, was massive.

I do take full responsibility for what I did, and I am honored by the people who showed up to support me in all ways. I can tell you that I was not on my best behavior at times. I would go back and forth like a scared woman, but sometimes my true self would emerge.

I could not meet the needs financially to cover the cost for both events. I knew I was in trouble. Most spiritual conferences do seem to struggle financially, and in the past, I had always been able to turn the corner in some way. I assumed these two would be no different. After all, I was serving the highest good. Wouldn't the Universe rush forth to support me?

But this time, that did not happen. The first conference came about and financially was not a success. My energy AND my bank account were drained!

I was able to have both conferences in 2009. That was a miracle in itself. I tried to cancel the second event but was unable. I had signed binding contracts with teachers, vendors, caterers, lodgings, etc, etc, etc. I had no choice but to go forward, knowing things were very, very wrong. The numbers were not adding up to financially support both venues.

I learned so much and put all of my heart and soul into the events. I believed in them. I had the best people working with me and up to a hundred volunteers helping me as well. Folks from Texas to California to Arizona and all over the world were helping.

The events were bigger than me. I was extremely exhausted, working fourteen-hour days, but my work was fear-driven, and the resulting vibration was also of fear. I was so afraid of our inability to fill the seats at the events.

Once both events were over, I collapsed. I was so tired that I was numb. I could not feel anything. Then came the roller coaster of feelings. I was feeling everything from pain to relief, and then back to sadness. I had to forgive myself and anyone I felt I had hurt or who had hurt me. I was also feeling guilty. I had hurt many during this time and asked for their forgiveness in meditation and in person.

I have been a student of A Course in Miracles for over fifteen years. I knew from all my study that I could not heal until I did some major forgiveness with the events and with myself and anyone involved in the events. My intention was to prosper in all ways, take care of all the details, and to pay off the energetic and the financial debts I had amassed. I was working in that direction, and I had no reason to doubt that I would be able to pull it off.

From May until August, I regained my energy to move around again with ease. While I healed and did the forgiveness work, and my energy started to flow again, I was also talking to professionals to see what I could do to restore my finances. I had not made up my mind yet about what to do—how to recover financially and energetically. I had to do these events and remember the gifts I learned from them, because there were so many. On the outside of these events, everyone involved loved them. They were very professional and top notch.

In August, my son James moved back home to work in Phoenix. Then, just when I seemed to be back on the energetic healing *wagon, tragedy struck. Sometimes it takes real tragedy, which has nothing at all to do with money, to jolt you into the remembrance of what is important. It is our relationship with those we love that sustains us—money is not our source.*

On August 23, 2009, my son was a serious car accident. The driver of the car had fallen asleep going eighty miles an hour on the freeway. The car had flipped eight times, landing in the middle dirt divider, miraculously not hitting any other car. All four of the kids in the car were airlifted to hospitals. All four kids made it, but my son was injured the worst. In the aftermath, his body medically "died." James' body was resuscitated. His neck was badly twisted and he was in a coma for two weeks. The doctors did not know if his body would pull through, so they prepared me for the worst.

I started to talk to James, to his Higher Self. During that time, it was my only relief. I spoke directly to James, and I felt as if I bargained with him to keep him here on the planet. I called all of my friends who are healers to work on him. Thank God all of them helped. James ended up making the decision to stay here on the planet. I know it had to be a big decision on his part. Now that it is behind us, I can see how big a decision it had to be. There were so many months of pain for his body. On that level, he had to know what a long recovery he would be enduring.

The doctors had to put a halo on him so that he would not injure himself. When we think of a halo, we see a wonderful ring of light around the head of an angel. The device called a halo in medical terms is much less comforting. It resembles a cage around the head of a patient and is used to manage cervical spine injuries to minimize neurological damage. One look at that device around my child's head was enough to communicate that we were in for a long recovery.

I was devastated—in deep pain and struggle. Here I was trying to figure out what to do with all of the expenses I had with the events. I simply had to put everything on hold, block it all out, and just be with my son.

It took seven months to get him out of the deepest part of the danger. His neck doctor called him the "walking dead." He had to have surgery on his neck in December, and the doctors were not sure if it would be successful. On the brighter side, James' right arm was completely shattered and the rods in his arm were healing very nicely.

By March, James was out of the woods. The operation worked! I was in shock for most of the recovery time. I was so afraid that James would leave the planet. I knew he was in fear as well. I felt such love for my son. During this time, his emotions were all over the place as well. I would go from sheer panic to working my spiritual studies, which included meditating, journalling and reading, "A Course In Miracles."

Sometimes I would think, Why is this all happening? I was so confused playing the victim role. I would find relief in friends. They would help me understand that recovery was happening. I could not make full sense of it all, so I agreed to stop analyzing it. I started putting all my energy into how I could move forward. Before this, I was immersed in survival mode. Most of my friends did not know what to say. Everyone around me seemed to be in shock. The events *of my life over the last few years threw us all into shock. For someone who always seemed to have the answers, it seemed I was at a loss.*

During this time, I found great comfort in my closest friend, Jane, and in my work with my clients. As a medium and an intuitive, I filled my days counseling and coaching those who came seeking answers in their own lives. It seemed the more I helped others see truth, the more I found it myself. The more I helped others find their answers, the more I found my own. When I was coaching or doing readings, it took me out of what was happening at home.

Jane's mother gave me some advice that helped immensely. "Treat James like the accident never happened." That one statement changed my energy and my vibration about the accident. It took me out of the vibration of fear. Once I was able to move out of fear, I was able to help James move through his own emotions, and the healing process could begin mentally as well as physically.

I am so grateful to tell you that James has fully recovered from the accident. I thank God for his recovery. James and I worked through our emotions and now we are both moving forward. That year was a very difficult year for both mother and son. We are so glad to have moved on and we are both finding our way now. It has changed us for the rest of our lives.

For me to start coming out of the pain and struggle for the last few years, I decided to let go of trying to understand it all. I owned responsibility on my part for the conferences and the toll it took on me. I forgave myself and everyone and asked for forgiveness as well. I decided I did not want to be in the victim energy anymore. I also knew that not forgiving would create self-punishment for me! I did not want to be punished, and it came to a simple decision. I moved out of it. I became very, very patient. I told myself that however long it took for the external to catch up with my inner peace, I would be okay with it. I did a key affirmation every day, "I am determined to be happy no matter what the external looks like."

And now, James is recovering, I am recovering, and this book appears to be a part of a full recovery. Helping others has always been what I do best, and William has come to help us all make a full recovery!

So William, do we all go through changes to change?

Yes, everyone does. It is set up that way so that you can grow soulfully and spiritually. It is designed that way because you require a bump in the road sometimes to move forward. Now WE know that love is changeless, and it is. However, your planet, as it vibrates at the level it does, is not vibrating at the level where the changes are not necessary.

With the evolution of your species, as such, changes are taking place and those changes are saving your souls, calling you to stay true to who you really are. It is true that the pain that most of you go through changes the charge in your energy to a higher vibration or to a lower vibration. WE are rooting for the higher for all of you. To understand this better, Tammy, do you know and believe you are not the same person you were two years ago and you never will be? It is when someone loses a loved one, changes jobs, or moves to another city that he/she is not the same person.

I get that on a really deep level.

Grand. The motto is: *You will learn it now or later, and you will learn it through joy or pain.* Those choices are up to you. You alone are responsible for that. Do not be like many who carry the energy to their deathbeds. Change it now while you are still in bodies that can live happy lives and you can create joyful, even blissful lives. Live lives without regrets; show the possibilities of what true happiness can be.

Another example of struggle and pain is not being patient in trusting God's timing. Patience is more than a virtue—it is accepting all is perfect. Most of you do not like to wait and much pain can come from just waiting for things to fall into place on their own. One of the key points is that it takes time for the external to show your inner changes. Most of the time, you are not patient enough to wait for the results to show up. So you go back to your victim role all over again. Sometimes you can get stuck and you do not even move forward. You get your signs of when to move things, but most of you do not move things until the Universe moves it for you. Tammy, tell them about your client who did not know if she needed to quit her job or not.

One of my clients called me years ago because she was not sure if she should quit her job. Tina's environment had gotten so bad that they had physically put her desk out into the hallway away from the other workers and no one was helping her out. HR would not look at it; she had gone to her boss to ask what to do, and there was no response.

My advice was to quit the next day and to trust the Universe to open a new job up for her. Her fear was such she could not even look at what was happening to her. She did quit the next day and the following week, a neighbor told her of a job that had just opened in her department and that her resume fit the job perfectly. Tina got the job making twice the money she was making and her desk was in a beautiful office space near others.

Sometimes when things are not working and they are not moving the way they should be—even though you may be pushing and pulling—it is because it is not supposed to move. **You** are supposed to move. The situation is not moving. **You** are the situation, and it is your place to change it. Getting so consumed in the problem is not solving it. Moving things around does not make the problem disappear. Remember, if the problem is still present, you are the problem.

Most of the time, you are not objective enough to see the solution. If you cannot find the solution and the peace within, or if you can't stop thinking about the it, than you become obsessive. Then you know you are in a rut. The pain can be very real to you, so the best thing to do is own that you are not in your right mind and ask for a change. It can help to ask, *What am I supposed to learn from this experience?* Changing the patterns can take a long time or they can take a few days or months to change. It really is up to you.

It is so interesting to see humans as they continue to struggle to the point it starts to affect the body. Once you reach a point where the body cannot take any more energy of pain and struggle, it starts to break down. That is why when so many people go through difficult times, extremely difficult times, their lives completely change. It is because the inner psyche is screaming for change and is going to get it one way or another.

That is why if you do not leave a job that is toxic for you, it becomes toxic to you. When you witness people crying as they pull up in their car to a job they dislike, it becomes more than a problem. This is the time to quit the job. Most people do not quit. They stay, thinking their security is in the paycheck. The true statement is you are your paycheck, not the job. Tammy, tell them about your client Debbie.

Debbie came to me two years ago and was very sick. I wanted to know why she was so sick. I asked her, and she did know. She told me that she had been at her job for twenty years and was not happy there but did not want to leave as she only had five years to go to retire. I told her that from her sickness, it was already apparent that she should quit this job immediately. There was no way she would make it five more years or even five more months.

There were so many things at Debbie's work that haunted her. Debbie vomited just thinking of being there. I advised her that it would be healthier for her to quit, but Debbie had more fear in leaving. She was more afraid of change and the unknown possibilities of a new way of earning a living. I heard about four months later that Debbie died from a heart attack. I still feel that if she had left that job, she would not have left the planet. But in the end, it was her choice. Had she realized the real choice she was making, she might have chosen to do things differently. Fear kept her from seeing what she really had to be concerned about.

I also had a chance to meet a young woman who was going to cosmetology school. When I talked to her, she was very depressed. I asked her what the root of her depression was, and she did know. This young woman told me she did not want to do hair at all. She wanted to become a backstage hand for a theater company and to learn everything about the theater.

My first question was, "Why are you not doing that?" She said her mom told she had to complete the training for the cosmetology school in order to work as a cosmetologist to pay back the loans that she had taken out to send her to school. There was more fear with money than doing what she wanted to do. This young woman was not listening to her intuition, which caused her depression.

I advised her mom to take her to theater school. If it were for her highest good, the money would work itself out. So the mom took her daughter to the theater that day and, to her surprise, one of the mom's old high school friends ran the program and was eager to help her daughter get into theater. The next day the loans from the cosmetology school were transferred to the theater school. To this day, the daughter is thriving and traveling around the world with the theater company. To no one's surprise, she is no longer depressed.

Because this young women knew deep within her soul that she was not doing what made her heart sing and was willing to change it, everything started to change for her. You know that saying, *This too shall pass*? What that means is that once you pass the experience of pain within you, then the outer experience will pass as well. It is all connected inwardly to the outer realm you live in. What is showing visibly is showing a reflection of your inward feelings.

From what WE are witnessing, if you can pull yourself out of your emotions for seconds at a time and be objective to what you are experiencing—the pain and struggle—you can then start to see you have options. As you wallow in your pain and struggle, you cannot think in your right mind.

If everything is judged as good or bad. It overrides every decision you make. Judging anything is fear-based, and you all do it so well.

Once you are in a judgment about yourself or someone else, this enslaves you to blame. Attacking or blaming someone else or yourself is a punishment cycle. There is no peace in this cycle, and it becomes like a insidious infection that grows very quickly. It is a persistent ache that festers and reminds you constantly why you are judging. You feel you have a right to judge what you are judging. Now remember, WE are talking to you about the struggles and pain you create. As the Course says, there is no order of difficulties in miracles and one is no bigger than the other.

When reading this, some of you may be thinking, "This is hard to read." But really, I'm just describing the patterns and cycles you have set up for yourself when things do not work out the way you think they should.

The truth is, things are working out beautifully in your best interests, and something better is in store for you to experience. Haven't you all had the experience of not getting a job you really wanted, and then a few weeks or a few months later, something even better came in because you had a few seconds to open up and accept that new possibility? All of you can think of a situation that did not work out the way you wanted and later you realized that it really had worked out even better for you. Some of you are flexible to changes and some of you are not.

Tammy had this happen to her in 1991 when she really wanted a job at a probation department. She got to the point where she put pressure on herself for the interview, and then she blew it! What really happened was that she learned of a different job a few weeks later at a refinery that served her well and paid off.

Tammy had a moment when she accepted that she might be of better service somewhere else—and where could that be? She put the intention out there that whatever happened was for her highest good. She was ready to bring in that job. That is all she did, and a miracle appeared.

The power of healing is on hand to heal anything. A Course in Miracles teaches us that all miracles are natural and everyone is entitled to them. You are no exception to the rule.

Now moving onto another cycle of pain, denial and guilt. Once you are in a cycle of denial and guilt your ego will require that you will punish yourself or others. No one is free from punishment in this cycle. Denial of any kind is also a dangerous way to live. A lot of people are in denial, but at the core of their being, they know when they are in trouble. WE want to say that as much as denial is dangerous, the truth is that it is important to listen to your inner self. Everyone knows when things need to be examined, but avoidance is the real culprit. Avoidance is dangerous. You will do anything to avoid dealing with the problem you think you have. So this creates more problems. The first problem creates another, and then another until you are so bogged down you cannot handle anything.

Now this is hard.

Repair your <u>errors</u>. Go make amends to those you feel you have wronged. The guilt comes from not repairing the act you feel you have done wrong. Making amends is a very healing event that also heals many. Redemption is a marvelous thing.

I had a client from Colorado who flew down to Phoenix to see me. Her son committed suicide. She was so upset over her son's death that three people had to carry her into my office because she was so distraught. When she arrived, I had her son with me in spirit. I knew his name, what had happened and why he came to the decision that suicide was the only way out for him. For hours the two of them talked through me. I do not remember what happened while they spoke. I do know that this lady walked out of my office happier and with answers. She no longer felt like she had caused her son to die.

No one is guilty of anything, we all make personal choices. Each soul has its own ability to die or take its own life. You choose even when you die. There are no victims even in our death cycles.

Another way of experiencing pain and struggle is through jealously, which is a vibration of thoughts and feelings of being deprived or lacking something within yourself. Your wrong mind thinking will have you looking externally as to why you are resentful that somebody has something you don't. Once you start to compare yourself, your ego has taken over. You are envious of what someone has or has done.

Ask yourself, "Why do I feel this way, and how can I embrace my own worth and ability to receive joy and love?" Once you are living in joy, love, and self acceptance, all jealousy vanishes.

William, I have seen this in a client who did not get the big promotion at work when he thought he should have gotten it. I also had a friend who was so upset because her friend was given everything—a house, a car, and a full scholarship to college; she was so jealous and felt life was not fair to her.

Tammy, what has happened is that the client who did not get the promotion did not get it because it was not his to have; his vibration was not aligned to receive the promotion he wanted. He also had many other things coming into his life at that time which required more of his personal attention.

Like what?

His family, friends, and his community. He already had the biggest deal happening in his life, if he could just see it.

So you are saying he is perfectly aligned with the deals that he was already creating? I do see that with him as well.

Yes, that is what WE are saying. He already has his deal working for him. The more he knows that his experience is brilliant and magnificent, other deals and projects will appear.

I get it. Embrace what is happening right now in your life because it is perfect and in alignment with your greatness.

Yes, that is it. You are the deal, the big deal.

Nicely put.

For your friend who feels like life is not fair because everything is handed to her friend and she is jealous, this play is perfect for both of them too. Your friend is finding her way and she will discover what she wants to do in schooling. Has she not been provided for, even with her schooling cost?

Yes, she is taken care of by her family who love her deeply.

As for her friend, who has everything given to her, this is perfect for her as well. This frees her up to educate herself and to start helping others sooner rather than later. That is all this is. Whether one life is different from another or one has more material things or education is irrelevant. What are you willing to do to create what makes you happy? Besides thoughts and feelings, are you willing to work, to master what's required, to be the best you can be? That takes courage, a strong conviction, and a willingness to allow all of that to seed within you.

The ego will measure everything it can, however love has no need to be measured. What is true is the love between them, only the connection is real and that is all that matters. Comparing anyone's journey to your own is the ego placing value on the valueless. Your value does not compare to another's journey ever, because they are you and their value is the same; there is no difference in any way. This is the ego distracting you into false thinking about yourself.

The next pain and struggle WE see constantly is the ego parts of you believing in who you are not. You try to play small and that frequency causes much pain, because you are not small. This is an example of not allowing your love in.

WE see you so small by things around you. You are not your fears, your stories, your wounds, your neuroses, your families, your pets, your clothes, your cars, your jobs, your houses or even your bodies. You are Light. You have a purpose of joy and service to others and to your planet. You were created to be that Light. The Course in Miracles says you separated yourself from God and forgot to laugh. Now what are you going to do about that?

Wake up from your dreams! Dare to say, *"No more pain or strife!"* Ask for another way. Stop the ride.

William, you are on a roll.

Yes, WE are eager to get your book done and without any hesitation. Moving forward, WE have such passion and light to see you thrive and not to be in strife anymore. Do you get it?

Yes, I think I do. What else do we need to talk about?

Another form of struggle is not allowing love into your lives. Some people are so afraid of love that they keep everyone away, and that is a cause for much pain. You are born into bodies to have relationships with each other, and some of you create stories of pain about how someone can hurt you, so you shut everyone out. Your heart's desire is to share your life with others in all forms and in all contents to experience love. As much as this is painful, how about allowing yourself to love others?

WE all know those who have loved and told themselves they will never love again. Who really is hurting here? Not allowing yourself to love again is a revocable punishment that has no goal but to punish you. WE know it is not easy when you lose someone as he or she crosses over, but why shut yourself off from having love again?

Have the courage to say that if there is anyone else out there for me, and it is for the highest good for both of us to meet, then let it happen. What if there were a great guy or gal waiting for you to open that door, but you just sat there and did nothing? That is what it is like when you hold yourself back. Remember, holding you back holds everyone back. It is plain and simple. What are you holding back from? The form is irrelevant. As Tammy says, there is only one of us here. If you are not moving forward into the Light, no one else is either. You are all a collective Light as one, and as you move forward, you move the whole Light of your planet forward. What are you waiting for?

Let's get real here—your planet is regressing, not progressing into the Light. You move four steps forward and five steps back. What will motivate you to step into your greatness and purpose and to be of service to the Light?

Tammy, tell them about your sister. This is an example of a soul that has gone through the cycle of pain and has come out of it much brighter, happier, and living her true self.

My sister Diana was part owner of a large mortgage company named Lending Tree. Early one morning, before she started Lending Tree, I called her about a dream I had. I informed her that a new business partner would call her within the hour to start a brand new lending company in California. I wanted to make sure she did not miss this wonderful opportunity. Now, you must know my sister and I are not morning people. For me to get up that early—before seven—to call her and for her to even answer the phone is a miracle. I proceeded to tell her that it would be one of the largest lending companies and it would take five years for it to be what she wanted. My sister put everything into building Lending Tree, to the point that she lost her identity and her joy.

Diana has lived most of her life as a workaholic and has taken care of many men financially in this lifetime. Her body was starting to show signs of stress, disease and pain. At the highest point of her career of over thirty years, she had the money to show for her work. She had over fifteen hundred franchises, but not the love in her life. I knew she was not happy, but she had no time to change it.

The soul part of her changed it for her. Her company went down like a lead balloon and she lost everything. Her husband left her for another woman, who happened to be her assistant, and her body was sick at that time. My sister went to stay with our mother for almost a year and a half. Our family was the only thing she could count on.

So, to say my sister was in her pain and struggle cycle is an understatement. She cried every day and released her pain in her tears. We all love her so much. I talked her into coming to Phoenix to be near me and she did. It took another year for her to start breathing easier and to believe maybe there was another way. During the two years she was down, she experienced the most healing that she had done in her whole life, and it served her well.

We were all so pleased to see her progress. It was as if she had nine lives. She was a wilted flower that bloomed again. Never underestimate the power of love and the power of releasing your pain. Now that she was doing better, she still wanted love in her life. I told her to set the intention that she was ready to receive love and to be taken care of, as well as to be able to take care of and love someone else. She started to say this, not every day, but enough that she started to believe it. Once that thought was planted in her mind and she was feeling love again for herself, I signed her up for an online dating service and she started dating again.

I advised her that until she knew who she really wanted to be with, she should just enjoy herself. I told her that her pilot light was lit again. She dated a handful of guys, and she was really having a great time.

Then one day she found Don. Their first date was a weekend in Flagstaff, Arizona. She brought him to my house that Sunday morning right after that date. While Don was in the kitchen waiting for my sister and I to come out of the bedroom, my sister and I were jumping up and down with joy and laughter because we both knew he was the one for her. She is living her love now for the first time in her life.

My sister's choices in men up until this time were not always the best. Mom had a few words for me when she found out my involvement in sis's new dating choices. But I knew that her dating choices were not based on the old faulty patterns she had accepted in the past and that this decision was a healthy one I assured my mother the choice was a good one, and she needed to trust Diana's decisions. Don is the guy—the love she was waiting for her whole life. I think now, Mom loves him more than my sister. We all love Don!

I was the Maid of Honor at their wedding! Now, I dance in my heart for her joy. When she passes, I will cry because of the love I have for her, not because she did not have a joyful life. It comes down to what we think we want is not what we really need. I do believe A Course In Miracles sums it up. We are like kids playing with scissors. We do not know what is in our own best interest. I always share this story with those who have given up on love. It illustrates that everyone can find love. Her life changed from one simple intention. If my sister can do this, so can anybody else.

Tammy, that is a great story.

Yes, it is.

It brings me to another subject that is troubling at best. It is the thought that many of you are not allowing yourself to receive love. You still believe that it must be earned, bargained for. Love is not earned or bargained for. Your worth is more than that, but you feel you are not worthy—more than that, many do not know how to receive it or live a love like that. Love is changeless, present, felt and has no outer requirements. You do not have to work for it, look a certain way, be young or old enough, or even totally heal to receive it. Once you know you are ready to receive it, it will happen.

What are you ready to receive within your experiences? Can you say you are ready to receive love and to be taken care of like Diana? Or is the concept so abstract that you do not even know how to incorporate it into your life? So many of you are trying to fill a void within yourself by looking outside of you to feel better. This is not love at all. Your ego has you looking outwardly when you should be feeling and loving yourself inwardly. You do not have to look for love at all, because as you are love, love will find you.

If you are not embracing your own love and you are looking too hard to find it, you have a one hundred percent chance of having more painful experiences. Love is content and not form. What this means is that the more you are coming from unconditional love, the more the connection is from within you to within another soul. Love is expressed and being aware of everyone's inner beauty. The form is ego-based and is constantly conditional to the external facts. The more you love yourself (and WE know this sounds "new age" to the realistic side of you), the more you are able to love others.

That is what Diana did, and so did Tammy. What is really interesting is that Tammy helped Diana to find love once she loved herself again. Tammy does not know this, but because she was with Diana, watching her unravel her life back into love, Tammy started to believe again as well. So within three weeks of Tammy's sister finding love, so did Tammy.

I have not thought of it that way.

Actually, that is the best way of explaining that when you find love, self, joy, passion in others, you bring it full circle back to you. Tammy's journey into believing it for her sister created it for herself, without her even knowing she was doing this. When you truly believe in someone else's happiness, love, joy, and passion, you will automatically bring it back to you, because love is endless—and that is the miracle.

Ok, I like that.

Love is more than the answer to all of you; it is the only way back home within yourselves. Tammy's story of her sister is a true testament that love does heal and create miracles for others in every way. Love is not based on time, place, your stories, your deserving-ness or even your makeup. It is based on you and your essences.

Until you believe in love, know you are love and allow love in, you will be away from it. You will experience anything but love, but from time to time, you will get a glimpse of it and it will beckon you back to it. Tammy, your heart is anew again—live that way.

I feel it, William, and I had to go through a lot to feel that. I do not wish that on anyone else.

No, you should not do that either. What you think will come back to you as good or bad. So keep creating loving thoughts.

I am willing to do that.

Now moving on to a slogan we like—equal opportunity employer. You are all equal in the eyes of God, and to your higher selfs. Equal opportunity employer, that is your inheritance, your birth right.

What?

Listen: equal opportunity employer. You all have the same equal opportunity to succeed.

What do you mean by that?

It does not matter where you came from, what you look like, what IQ you have, in order to be successful. If you are not where you want to be, you cannot say it is because of any other reason than yourself. Look, you have an African American president; you almost had a woman president. (That will happen later around 2018.)

What will happen? A women president?

Yes, and you already have women leaders in other countries. What WE are saying is the world is your oyster, and you can be anything you want to be. It is based on your skills, what you are willing to believe in, and also what you incarnated to be.

Ok, so what are you saying here?

Rising above your little self is the key. What are you passionate about being? What are you passionate about doing? Set forth into that direction. Find out anything you can about it, move towards it, and be patient for it to manifest. This is another painful experience WE see people are not following their passions. So many say, "*I do not know what to do, I am lost, confused and baffled.*"

That is not true. Everyone knows what to do. Most are so afraid of failure and the notion that they are their smallness, it holds up everything. Then you believe you are not worth it either. Or you put yourself out of your comfort zone and freak out. So what will it be? Will you play with a full deck or play with what you are dealt? Move on. Get out of your way and be sane enough to dare some joy and passion. If you love trains and enjoy making them or putting them together, start doing that again.

What?

Do what you love, even when you are working. Add some joy. Go back to being child-like again. Go back to what brings you joy. When is the last time you smiled? When is the last time you really smiled?

Hmm.

Exactly. Go find that innocence again. That energy will change this world you live in, not the fear or the doubt or the judgments.

What is also interesting are these two things: The first one is that you can talk to anyone at any time through mediation and prayer. WE see collectively that more people are using that modem now. WE celebrate with you as you connect to Source.

The second thing is that over a hundred years ago there were not so many people on the planet as compared to over 6 billion people today. *Why is that,* you ask? Because there is so much darkness, many souls are eager to incarnate to help shift the energy to Light. The newer incarnations are geared to change quicker into the Light. It is taking more souls to shift your planet to light than it did ten years ago.

I bet. So you are saying the younger incarnations get it?

Yes, they do, but what they do with it is their choice.

William, there are many who are Lightworkers who are doing their practices and sharing what they know with others.

There are many Lightworkers and many incredible souls working to change the planet. As this book is written, some of those souls are tired and have done the journey and work for many years.

Yes, but if we keep connecting to the Holy Spirit, then it replenishes our souls and spirits.

What is needed is more self-care for all humankind. That is part of the struggle as well. Most humans do not know how to give back to themselves. With all of the busy-ness of your world, it is getting harder for people to slow down to meditate, reflect—or even process. Remember how many clients you have had to give homework to, to get them to just sit for fifteen minutes a day to be with themselves? You told them no TV, phones, radio or any interferences.

Yes, I do remember that. I worked with some who have never been able to be with themselves and did not have healthy relationships. The patterns were showing up as addictions or reaching out desperately for a new partner to fill their voids. It was pretty hard for many of them to just sit still. They wanted desperately to have loving relationships. Once they started doing this, everything fell into place, and they are doing very well.

If you are not comfortable being with yourself, can you see the cycles of pain in that? Everyone has a wonderful opportunity to be with themselves, and even if it feels painful at first, it will alleviate after a few times alone. Checking in with yourself and spending time alone sometimes is very soothing to your soul. Now on the other hand, some people spend too much time alone. It requires a check from time to time to see if you are happy—and you always know the answers to this.

If you do not like being with yourself, this is a warning that you are running from you. You can never run from yourself. At some point in your life, you will choose peace or you will exit. Have you noticed most humans who are ready to cross over start the separation process before they leave? Your life is worth sharing and exchanging. That is what you came here to do.

As for those who do not reach out to others, it is from a false sense of believing they can be hurt. In truth, they are already hurting. Your experience on Earth is to share your time with others, not to isolate yourself. As Tammy has heard over and over again, do you want to be happy or do you want to be right? This is really self-care, giving time to yourself as well as blending in with others. Being enlightened is being a part of your community and sharing your wisdom and your kindness.

WE will give examples later about how to do that. Also, the thought that because you are spiritual and someone else is Methodist or a Mormon or an atheist, it does not mean they are not Light. Everyone is Light! There are more than a 1000 ways to find self, love, God, Buddha, empowerment or whatever you want to call it. All walks are in Divine Order and lead you to love.

The key is to be diligent. It takes a daily practice to find it, to sustain it and vibrate at a higher level. The idea of doing a practice every day is very hard for people, and that creates more problems, even for the most dedicated individuals. Please do not get so hung up on the form that others take to find their way. It is not your place to project your beliefs onto others. Your way is not the only way. Your way of living is not the only way either.

I know that too. So why is it then that your life matters?

Because you're placed exactly where you need to be to matter to those in that same place who have your beliefs and your purpose.

I get that.

WE see many who create pain and struggle by having expectations of how your relationships should be or not be. All relationships are for loving and a way to communicate love. Your interpretation of what relationships look like or how they can benefit you are not coming from love at all. Relationships are there for you to embrace each other unconditionally without any expectations or anything in return. Also, when you are attached to the form of the relationship and not allowing the relationship to be what love calls it to be, your interest is not love, it is manipulation.

I can see what happens, William, when I have not talked to you. I've had a few hard days lately.

Yes, that is because you got caught up in judgment, did you not?

Yes. Can we move forward?

Yes, that is what we are doing.

Thank you.

You're welcome.

It is interesting that over a hundred years ago, many were in pain because they would move away, never to see their loved ones again. Because of the times, their limited transportation and phones were not there, the way they are now. So many of those years were spent in pain because they physically could not talk to their loved ones except by mail and that took weeks to months.

People do not have that problem so much now. Now your family either lives nearby or you can take a plane to see them, so there is no stopping you from seeing your family members. Now WE also know that sometimes it is better not to be around certain family members. That is a personal call.

What WE are seeing is that there are many people too busy to make time to see their loved ones. That is another example of pain and struggle. You know you need to go, but you do not. That inner voice can tell you, *"I really need to go see them."* Not listening is a cause for pain.

What are your benefits? What are the benefits from suffering? What WE also see is that some people get a lot of attention from pain and drama. It creates a distraction from being responsible. Some families set up shop with this. The kids act just like them. There may be one or two in the family dynamic who are not caught up in the cycle. What do you think happens to that member? He or she shifts to another group of friends because they do NOT act that way.

So the drama and the suffering is all an ACT. ACT—Acute Crazy Transference. An ACT from the ego to keep you crazy. You all know of families who are like this. Some people stay stuck in the drama because they are afraid of losing their loved ones. They will sacrifice their journey's purpose and happiness just to be with someone. You call this love?

Let's talk about couples. How many couples stay together when one of them knows he or she should not be with the other person? When one person in the relationship starts to evolve and change, the reality is that both parties know this is happening and it can cause much fear. One of the parties will start to get uncomfortable with the changes and will demand that the other one stay the same way. The real truth of this is that the relationship has been successful, learned what was needed and now it is time to move on.

WE want to recognize a couple as two people coming together whether it is a man and a woman, or a man and a man, or woman and a woman. The forms of the two bodies do not matter. Love is love, period. The judgment that your planet holds about who is with who does not matter. It does not matter if one believes differently in religion or one is black and one is white or one is Mexican or one is Asian. It is a soul loving another soul.

Love is energy. Why is there judgement when you love someone? If your kids or parents or friends are HAPPY with who they are with, why can't you be HAPPY too? HAPPY— Holding Absolute Peacefulness Presently Yours. To abandon someone because you do not like the choice of who that person loves is you <u>ACT</u>ing and projecting your fears. The kicker is that the pain and struggle this is causing you will cause the one who is judging—you—to lose out in the end. Not everyone believes the way you do and never will. The circumstances of your life are not a cookie cutter for everyone else's. WE are all different personalities living on one planet.

There are also couples who do stay together for most of their lives, and they have no problem allowing each other to grow. It is like a swim of energy that weaves back and forth throughout their marriage—a testament of a joyful union.

Another form of struggle WE witness is when there are custody battles over children. What is really interesting is that the courts are doing the best they can by giving both parents the opportunity to see their children. The offset of this is that half of the custody battles get lost in the system.

What is needed is some counseling sessions before mediation, because WE witness most parents using kids like properties when negotiating who has ownership of the children. The struggle and pain is delusional and a real experience for both parties. What is best for the kid(s) is the answer. Fighting over anything is destructive and the emotional toll it takes on the children is evident in your world. The damage creates ripples of tears in the child's makeup.

So what WE are saying is staying in a relationship too long causes much pain and ending relationships creates pain as well. It does not have to be this way, if you can see it differently. You can ask yourself how you can accept the change with the form of the relationship you are in.

What is needed is a new thought about ending relationships and how to share custody of the children. How can everyone win in this situation?

One of the other ways to have clarity in your relationships is by noticing what you are attracting into your life. The key here is not to get so caught up in the form of the job, house, friend, lovers, etc. What are you attracting into any area of your life and how are you feeling about it? Are you feeling peace, love for your job, home, friends, lovers, wife, husband, even kids? Take inventory of how you are feeling about it and own your feelings without judging yourself. Ask how you can see them differently.

Sometimes that is all it will take to change the play back to love again. The healing is the easy part. What is hard is the commitment to doing it. It also can be quite a change for you because it needs to change. The attachment to what you are doing is not working. Release the attachment to all you think you need, want, require, deserve, have—past, future, and even the present.

So the pain comes from our attachments?

Yes. Let go of all attachments to anything.

Sounds crazy!

No, it is not crazy. It is sane, because you are not hooked into anything at that point. The only hook you will have then is God, your Higher Self.

Ok, so how do you do that?

Letting go of your attachments, your thoughts, good or bad— as you say, your baggage—will start to shed life and Light again into yourself to allow a pure thought—there can be a brighter way.

Sometimes all it takes is owning it and the rest will shake out like a dirty rug that has been sitting on the floor too long. WE are coming from a place of the true observer, and WE can tell you by looking at all of you that your strife and struggles are unnecessary and easier to fix than you think.

The way that you are living on your planet is not working. Your time is NOW. NOW— New Opportunity at Winning—to change it. What excites you about waking up? What are you excited to see happen in your life?

You are pretty harsh here.

WE want to make sure you get the seriousness of your thoughts and actions. The ego is much more clever than you alone. Your only chance of changing is recognizing that you need help. Join with God, Truth and Holy Spirit to regain your joy again. This is the only way.

You are overly concerned about what others think of you, if you leave your job, cut your hair, move out of town, stand up for yourself. Stop thinking about what others think of you. The only thing that matters is what you think of you. What do you think and feel about you? You will always have someone who does not like you, and that is ok. There are always going to be people you do not like either. WE know you are probably thinking this information is too basic. Yes, it is, and that is where you are stuck—at the basics.

Accept yourself as you are. You are what you are. Struggles come from disliking your body, your life. You incarnated into the body you chose, the family you chose to be with, the community, the talents. Trust enough that this is for your highest good. It amazes us how some of you try to change your scripts. Change you and the scripts will change automatically for you to serve a higher vibration.

So, William, you are saying to honor your incarnation and to trust what was set up from the get-go. Out of our mother's womb?

Yes, that is what WE are saying. You chose to be born in Pittsburg, Pennsylvania. You also chose your mother and father and your siblings.

I really did pick the members of my entire family? Just kidding. I love my family.

That is another story of how many are grief-stricken with memories of family members and cannot let it go. You cannot change what happened to you in the past, and with much respect, at some point you have to be tired of the pain you are in. What can you do NOW to bring some hope, Light, healing into your life? If you do not have the answers, someone does. You cannot say that you do not have a way to contact someone to get what you need. Everyone on your planet is capable of getting any information needed with a touch of a finger.

Continuing on—your stories in your mind that are not loving at all, will always hold you back. Look at how you feel when you are thinking about a past story. How does it make you feel when you are selectively thinking about it? If any story from the past or present memory does not feel loving, then you know the energy from that story is not love but fear. You have a choice to release it or let it hold you back.

WE know this is intense reading for all of you. As the chapters unfold, WE will have much fun and even a joke or two. WE just want to emphasize how important it is to move past this dangerous cycle you call pain, the stories you hold on to that do not serve you or anyone else. The false stories that you make up create blocks and much unhappiness in your lives. You hold your past mistakes as beacons of roadblocks, thinking you will keep recreating the same outcomes. You can do that or you can change your thoughts about it.

Tammy, share the story about your client Linda. It is a real example of how a story can hold you back from love and joy.

Linda came to me about six years ago, and all she wanted was someone to love her. Linda had a nice life, home, great job and pretty good health. Her true desire was to be loved and to have companionship in her life.

I found out her fears were about relationships and her past. Linda had much fear around relationships. Her past three relationships had much pain, some physical abuse and some emotional abuse. I do believe that Linda was ready to heal her own wounds and her own pain habits. Linda took responsibility and forgave herself and the men in her past to the point she had no fear in her to create a new relationship.

Once the charge of her anger and hurt was gone, as I mentioned the three men from her past, I took Linda into a meditation to see her new man and there was no one there. I had to bring her out of the meditation to see what was happening. I found out that Linda had to announce and claim that she was willing to bring in a new man into her life with whom she could give and receive love, with the intention that it was a healthy, loving relationship.

In working with Linda, I found out from her guided meditation, that until she was willing to announce that she was willing to see things differently and allow herself to be healed from her past relationships, the outcome could not change.

Right after that, I took Linda back into the meditation and to her surprise, there was a man waiting to meet her. I had Linda feel the energy—what it felt like and what he looked like. For the next thirty days I had Linda connect to that guy. Linda felt safe and excited about the possibility of loving someone again. Within a year, she met a man and is now happily married. Because Linda was willing to let go of her story of her past and to not give it more power than needed, she changed her life.

Another area that causes pain and struggle is your worldly beliefs about money and the false power you give to it. Your source is YOU not the money. Money is only a form of exchange of a currency.

One of the biggest fears you have about money is, how can you spend it or hold onto it. It is all energy, and your intention around money is what guides the connection to your actions with it. It is really the leading cause of deaths on your planet. You will sacrifice everything for money or the lack of it. So you think it is cancer or another disease that is killing you? What do you think causes cancer or other diseases? Fear. Fear of anything. The number one cause of deaths is related to your relationship and thoughts about money. You will stay at a job that will kill you or you will take money from someone for yourself at their expense. I repeat, the number one fear—and this is the biggie—is your thoughts about money—period.

Your species will even kill for it or die for it. It comes down to whether you have enough money to pay for your hospital bills. WE have been shown that some people are refused treatment because of lack of money. Can you imagine the ripple effect of that for your planet? If you refuse treatment to someone who needs care, how is that going to touch others? Do you feel in alignment to your purpose? There is always a way to help someone who needs care, and working together creates more money. It is not the hoarding or the holding back. Money is just a currency to spread around to be exchanged for services or products. The energy behind it, set by you, is the substance that binds the money's energy. This energy comes from love or fear. You will either appreciate money or you will not.

Depression results from money being held up and not flowing through the channels. Holding anything back—money, love or joy— also holds that back for everyone else. I am talking about extremes here, but it is so common that you all give so much power to money and what it can and cannot do for you. It causes strife and pain, people not talking to each other, long term resentments with others. You give money more power than your relationships.

Tammy, tell them about some of the people you coach who experience a loved one's death and there is money to be divided.

I have coached over twenty clients after a loved one has died and in all twenty cases, the executor has not followed the will and the wishes of the deceased. I am just mentioning this because when people call me it is because there is a problem. I am aware that there are cases where the personal wishes of the deceased are followed, but I see the other side of that, when the wills are not followed. All of the relationships are shattered and changed. Those relationships do not recover until forgiveness and redemption are brought into play.

People call me when they want answers or are ready to heal. A third party is neutral and not attached to the outcome; it is much easier to see the solution. Because I am a student of "A Course in Miracles" and an intuitive, I have been able to coach over five thousand people and have read for over twenty-five thousand people since 1996. The gifts I have learned, and I am still learning from counseling and doing readings, are wisdom, love and compassion. The reality is that we are all one with the same issues and fears. I must say I am not special in any way. I do believe being an intuitive is not a gift but a muscle that you can use to obtain answers. The people I counsel, coach, and read for have been my saviors; they keep teaching me the truth and how to love.

So, William, what are you saying about money?

Money is not as evil as you think. What can be tainted is the thought that you cannot be without it and will do anything necessary to have it. The true statement is that your wealth is in your mind and hearts and not in the actual dollar. Connect within and the money will show up. There is an endless stream of money, and it is all there for all of you. Sacrificing is not love—it is fear-based. So any thought to sacrifice for money or anything else is destructive and a cause for unhappiness.

I know already you are thinking that you cannot live without money. Your system is set up that way. It is set up to operate from a system that is breaking down right now and all of you are witnesses to it. Connecting to your inner wisdom will bring you the money. It is the surest thing to count on. Most of you do not.

Taking the next step in discovering your higher self is allowing divine order to be placed in your life. A holy instant of order—where principle one is allowing the peace within and where you can shatter any pain and struggle.

WE are so excited to share with you how easy it is to move forward and to regain your joy and your vibrancy and the trueness of who you are. The principles are set up so easily that all you have to do is follow them. You can also witness the unfolding of your movement to a brighter you. Bear with us as WE continue to write this chapter and the following chapters; you will see the change in your own frequencies. You will discover living joy, passion and peace again.

Since you are reading this book, you are ready for change and a new beginning. New beginnings start every second. You can decide at any time to change things back to Divine Order. It is not that any situation is not in Divine Order, because it is.

What is not Divine Order are your reactions into fear. Only love is Divine Order at any time. The fear that emanates from not understanding a situation creates a series of consequences that denounce your truth and lead you into confusion. It is very interesting how so many try to understand something you cannot understand. Let it go for now and you will move out of Principle One quicker. The ego is very clever in keeping you down as long as possible.

Struggles and pain are not the most pleasant topics for all of you to read, however, they are the most important of the topics because until you can fully grasp Principle One, you cannot go into the other Principles. It is very similar to your first chakra—if you cannot clear it out, how can you move up to the others.

WE are talking a lot about pain and struggle for many reasons, because it is the first step in this chapter, and it is the first step and most important to move beyond. It is the hardest step to move past, and yet once you have moved through step one, the rest of the principles will be much easier. So please take note that the ego side of you will keep you trapped here as long as it can. Getting past the first principle can take seconds, minutes, years, and even eons if you allow it.

And know and believe that the forces of Light and love are more powerful. Just a few seconds of the Divine Energy going through your thoughts can change you back to Light in an instant. So things do change on a dime and your life can and should be transformed by one pure thought. You can lose everything and regain it.

The hope WE have and the thought WE carry for your planet is two-fold: first, that your Source will light you up to your truest selves so that you no longer need the separation from God; and second, that you remember your soul's purpose and the unity of Divine Love.

Given the time frame of your planet's cycle, WE predict that most of you will join us in these pure thoughts between now and one hundred years into the future. Know that even if you are incarnated again or living in spirit, your children and your children's children will witness and live in the higher vibration as well.

WE alone cannot do this. You are all needed to lift the veil and the frequencies to a higher vibration. As the saying goes, as you move forward, so do those around you. It is the same for us. As you move forward, WE move forward within you. Even if WE are not in bodies, our frequencies are all connected like webs that cross over into all dimensions and times.

41

So please, for the life of God in you, can you for just a moment lay down your burdens and be willing to ask for another way? There definitely is one. The other way is easier, lighter, fun, and playful. As Dr. Phil says (and WE like this saying), *"Is it working for you?"* You already know the answer to that.

Creating a space in your home that feeds your heart is vital to your journey. WE pray you all have a space that feeds you. Walk into a space that gives you the freedom to just say, "I love being here." Do you have that? WE are not concerned about the form of the place, just how you feel when you are in it. If you do not have such a space, WE suggest that you create it. One of the clearest places is in nature. Go there to just connect, to allow the vibration of nature to feed you so that you can align your thoughts again.

Is there anything else we need to talk about before we finish up Chapter One?

Your struggles are not what you think they are.

What do you mean?

WE know how difficult your last few years have been, but what you must know is that your struggle is from fear that you let a lot of people down; but most of all you feel you have let yourself down.

Yes, I do. I know I could have shown up better in many ways.

That is true, Tammy, but you cannot change what you did in the past.

I know that. So how can I see things differently?

You can by forgiving yourself. Stop punishing yourself, okay?

Okay, I can do that.

This is so essential to your journey. Say, "I now forgive myself and everything that I did to hurt anyone or myself up until this day. I now release all notions of obligations that are harmful to my well-being. I now give back to those with whom I have had transgressions. I ask that whatever is owed to them from my actions be given to them in kindness and love and retribution. I take responsibility for my actions and deeds and now ask the High Heavens to align my patterns back to their original state of Oneness with God. I release all negative thoughts and feelings I have placed on myself or anyone else to be reversed and transcended into the Light matter of unconditional love, hope, and wisdom."

I like that.

You should, it will save you.

I believe that. Now, is this going into the book?

Why not? It is you, representing me. Your struggle has been everyone's struggle. Allow yourself to be vulnerable and available to others. Love is showing all sides of yourself. Do you not agree?

I have not thought of it like that!

Tammy, you do know that as you are writing this, you are healing with it. You are gaining a newer version of yourself.

I am speechless and honored and deeply grateful.

You are welcome. Now back to this chapter as WE move into another topic that needs to be addressed.

Have you heard of the telepathy dialogue?

No.

Telepathy dialogue is part of your make up and how your true self communicates to others with or without you knowing.

You know, the thoughts you are thinking about someone else—it may be of love or fear. Most of you on your planet do not get it Every thought has power, measured over a thousand waves of making connection to others. So if you are sending a thought in a room to one person and you have judgment about that one person, over a thousand people will pick it up.

I get that, because sometimes I can send a thought and I know that a few people will pick up that same thought and feeling.

Exactly.

How does this apply to struggle and pain?

Because every thought has power to the point that if you sent out a thought that has much anger or judgment, it will ricochet that back to you a thousand times to validate your pain. That is why when someone is depressed or deeply sad, your thoughts of love are needed—and only love is needed.

I do understand.

To change yourself and someone else back to love is to become love, only love.

Now, the reversal is true as well. If you are sending only loving thoughts to someone, that vibration will come back a thousand fold to you as well. But added to that, the frequency of love that you send can deliver you and someone else from a lower thought pattern.

Can you give me an example?

Sure. Do you remember when you helped your sister-in-law by setting the intention on Christmas day that you were going to be with your family without judgment? You left all of your past thoughts at the door.

Remember how you felt after that Christmas day?

Yes I do. That was one of my best Christmases ever. I felt love and I still think of that from time to time.

Your sister-in-law was changed from that. Just ask her. You are not separate, and if anyone is crying for love, start with yourself and then move on to another and then to another.

What feeds your love, joy and happiness?

Your psyche is like a soul bank account, and WE apologize for the words WE are using. WE want to make this as simple as possible. If you feed your soul bank account with joy, fun, playfulness, and sharing love with others, it builds a strong Light and a strong base to your being-ness. Your Light has a way of connecting to Source to filter and replenish itself at the same time. Mixing it up a bit will better suit you.

Why is that?

As your species has demonstrated, you require different ways to be fed. You tend to get bored with doing the same thing every day and your pattern as a whole is to quit feeding yourself. So mix up your fun. Again, the form does not matter. Fill your soul bank account so that you have a reservoir to tap into.

Can you explain why it is so necessary for us to do this?

Because the frequency of your planet is not vibrating at the level to feed you alone. With a call for help and a willingness to regain your sanity, you are opening the Heavens to deliver you from lower-level thinking. As you do this, your connections with others will be holy, and your new energies will lift you above the battlefield.

I love how the Course says we are in a battlefield and we need to rise above it to change our thinking.

Yes, you are at the lower level. Your planet has many levels in itself, and your commitment should be to rise above the battlefield and higher into the universal wisdom level of the All Knowing. This lower-level vibration is where much pain and struggle lies. So do you want to stay there or move up?

I want to move up and stay up.

Ok, then feed your soul bank account to lift you. If all of you could see where you are on these different levels, then all of you would choose to do whatever you could to move up.

Wow, heavy duty stuff. I have to ask this question. How many levels are there?

There are six levels in your planet. The first two levels are the heaviest to be in. These are levels of despair, victimhood, hopelessness, grief.

Then the next level, the third, is where most of your population is. It is a level of getting by, doing what's in front of you. Having some fun from time to time, but just doing life as if you were a robot. WE see this a lot with people on your planet. They do the same thing over and over again. This is much better than the lower two; however, miracles are not experienced at this level. You are not really happy and not really sad.

Now, the forth level is one of having hope; believing again that things can be different. It is a place where you now believe that the story can actually change. You have such vigor and spring about you. You are moving differently. You are now the co-creator of your life.

I get that. That is a great place to be.

Yes it is, and you can move up even more.

The fifth level of your planet is where you go to tap into your Higher Selves. It is a place most of you go to when you meditate. Many speakers and musicians and creative minds tap into this to create great masterpieces of work. This state feeds your soul's bank account to over-flowing. It can carry you throughout your day and change lives. You feel alive and happy. Not much can bother you at this level. Most of you just want to soak it up. This is where others can feel the love and want to be around you.

I like that.

You use this level most of the time when you are teaching. That has been why you have made it so well over the last few years. Another insight, because the work you are doing with your clients has also come back to you in your soul's bank account.

I do love my clients, and I do see them differently until they can see themselves as wonderful as I see them. My clients have saved me in many ways.

The sixth level is one of transparent Divine Order for your global planet. This is one of the highest frequencies you can go to without leaving your body. At this level, you are feeling like you are here but you are not. You are vibrating in two realms. Remember when that has happened to you?

Yes I do. This has happened a few different times to me when I was speaking to an audience. I did not sleep for days, and I could not get enough water in my body. The audience was transformed and everyone had the same experience as I did. All of the electronics were shutting off and going on at the same time. I had to unplug all of the electronics in my hotel room.

Yes, and from that state, you are the miracle. You did not have to do anything but be that vibration.

Wow. I do not remember anything I said either. It took everything for me to just hang on. It was the most blissful, intense experience to date. Someone told me later that my aura was gold in color and that many miracles did happen from that engagement. But how did I get there? What were my thoughts?

Tammy, you were asking for another way and God showed you. You were open to the experience.

I felt it. I did alter into another frequency. But I could not sustain it.

Yes, you did. We are just reminding you of all the levels for those who need to picture where they are vibrating from, then that may give them a nudge to change.

So, on an average, what percentage of our population is at each level? What is it going to take to change our planet back to a higher frequency?

Loaded questions. To the best of our abilities, what WE see occurring the most is:

The first level is about 8 to 10 percent.

At the second level, about 12 to 15 percent.

Then the third level, about 64 to 67 percent.

The fourth level, about 12 to 16 percent.

The fifth level, about 4 to 8 percent.

The numbers vacillate as you move back and forth through the levels. So the numbers may not add up to 100 percent in each area. I know you are adding the numbers and it adds up to 100 percent.

Yes I did. That is so wild!

However, because there is a swing going on all the time, it may not be always 100 percent. Not everyone stays at one level all the time. Some do and some do not.

Sixth Level ———————————————— 22%

Fifth Level ———————————————— 4-8%

Fourth Level ———————————————— 12-16%

Third Level ———————————————— 64-67%

Second Level ———————————————— 12-15%

First Level ———————————————— 8-10%

To answer your second question about what is needed to change your planet to bring the Light and to have a higher percentage on the fourth and fifth level, once you are at the fourth level, this is where your Light will change others. It is a trick question because the numbers are not the issue here. It is how many people you can touch at this level. Remember that WE said you can touch a thousand people with one thought?

Yes.

At this level, you can touch millions with your energy. It will carry and can deliver many from their lower vibrations.

It sounds wonderful and hopeful.

Yes, this level is needed, because as you know, the fifth level is not consistent and you will either come back down out of it or you will transfer into the next level.

I do get that.

So what WE are saying is that in the fourth level, the numbers need to be higher. Yes, if WE can get the fourth level up to 22 percent at any given time, your planet would change drastically.

So we have our thoughts cut out for us. I do have another question about the levels. You said there are six levels and you have only talked about five of them. What happened to the sixth level?

WE wondered when you were going to catch that. The sixth level is the level of transference to another realm, another place.

What do you mean?

When your body dies, it can go into this level to be transported into another realm of existence. This level carries your soul and spirit into total transference of Light. You also transport into your new birth of existence—without your body, of course.

To sum up what we just talked about and look at the picture to explain it, this is just a summary of where you are all vibrating. From the information given, you should know exactly where you are vibrating. This will also take you out of struggle and pain.

WE are now coming to a conclusion for Chapter One and how you can regain peace within and move past the first principle. You are more than any fear thoughts or feelings the ego part of you would like you to live by. You are God, incarnated.

What, I am God?

Yes Tammy, you all are God—one hundred percent. I know you may not believe that totally as of yet. What percentage do you believe you are God? Ten? Twenty? Seventy? What part of you own that you are God? It is more than arrogant to denounce your God Selfs. It is ludicrous.

How do we own that?

By saying you are willing to embrace the God within you. Where do you think God lives?

Inside me.

Yes, now you are living your God Selfs.

Now WE know that the pain can be very real to you. WE also know that all of you have moments of truth that slip into your minds that can deliver you from your fears. WE know that your efforts and your consistent commitment to observing your thoughts will stop the pain.

As WE address many of the scenarios of pain and struggle, WE know you all have many to tap into, talk about, and feel, judge, and most of all, feel wounded about. Let's all be clear in knowing that if you were not ready to change this, you would not be reading this book. We applaud all of you for taking the first step in moving out of pain and struggle. We are gladdened to see your souls moving to joy again.

Be willing to see things differently. Ask God to help you to see not just some things differently but everything differently. This is the miracle—to master Principle One—to be open to thinking and seeing everything differently. You may have thought, is that it? Yes, it is because truth is simple. A simple heartfelt intention or prayer will deliver you from your pain and delusional thinking.

The first step is: Express your intention, by praying to the Holy Spirit, or call in your own belief by saying this: I now am willing to embrace my God Self, one hundred percent.

"I now surrender this (fill in the blank with your issue), to be transmuted back to love. I am willing to see my part play out differently for everyone to win. I take full responsibility for how I am feeling and acting. I now want to be happy and at peace again. I ask for Divine Order to take place in my mental, etheric, physical and spiritual well-being NOW."

Now are you all ready for Chapter Two?

More than you know. I think all of us are asking for easier times.

That is why you are writing this book: for everyone to move higher up into joy again.

Remembering One, Once Again

The 2nd Principle:
WHAT CAN I DO NOW?

Ask. The answers are available through love, intuition and guidance. Learn to be still and listen for them.

Looking at how you resolve your own fears is like jumping out of a plane without a parachute, thinking you will land safely. It seems that it is very difficult for all of you to surrender to a new way, a healthier, more serving way for yourselves.

The 2nd Principle is so simple in words, and yet most of you step back from exhaustion, beat down internally before you ask for help. If that is what it takes, then so be it. Or, you can just ask every day, *"What can I do now?"*

When you come to the point in your life where you do not have the answers, or get tired of trying to fix things, or bargain or beg for solutions, then you are coming into your right-mindedness.

This is a new way of resolving your fears—asking *"what can I do now?"*

A Course in Miracles came as an answer to the question, *There has to be another way. What is it?* It is huge that one sentence can change the direction of your life when it is filled with love, passion, reverence, purpose and deep conviction. It changes everything back to love again.

This chapter is about you taking responsibility because you are creating all of your experiences. You are finally aware that you have operated the ship and maybe on a few occasions have given the steering wheel over to God and have taken it back again.

Tammy's mantra for the last year has been, *"The more you are in God's will, you have no free will,"* because at that level you are living and breathing the Will of God. You would not want it any other way or maybe you can go back to Chapter One and start there all over again. I am guessing that since you are reading this, you do not desire that and want to learn from joy.

The term *love* is just a word. Can you really get into the meaning of the word *love*? What does love look like? The feeling of unconditional love is without expectations, without attachments, without conditions, without worries.

The answers come from just love. What can I do now from love and only love? LOVE—Living Open Vast Experiences of joy. You created your life down to your eye movements, your skin colors, and the hairs on the top of your head. That is a miracle.

If you had everything in place—perfect harmony, perfect home, perfect money, the perfect love, perfect relationships, health, family, purpose and a spiritual connection—what would you do from that place? That is the place where you choose your decisions, stop settling for less or sacrificing or playing martyr to anyone or anything.

William, it is really difficult to come from a place of having everything in alignment, especially when things are not reflecting that in the world.

Tammy, that is true. However, just try it out. You cannot lose anything just from trying it. Try starting today thinking you already have everything—how would that feel? Then, make your decision based on that and that alone. Let's face it: How is it working for you from the place you are currently making those decisions?

Not always that well.

Ok, then. That awareness should have you motivated to change directions first within yourself.

I know you are also thinking about how you are feeling about everything. Your feelings do play a huge part in driving you. You sometimes cannot think clearly about the directions of your lives. Put aside your emotions right now and soak in the words so they can resonate back into your thoughts correctly. It does take discipline and dedication to do this. Changing a pattern can be difficult, but the pattern will be more difficult.

Your planet and your species think that everything is difficult or hard or will take so much effort, so you stop yourself before you even get out of the gate. You give up way too soon. You lose patience and focus. One of the hardest traits to overcome is that you are only committed partly and most of the time that commitment is conditional.

What do you mean "conditional"?

Your commitments are mostly conditional with too many expectations. If the outer world is not playing out the way you want it to, then you give up, throw in the towel, or you go in another direction. Some of the best ideas or ways were done from things that people did not give up on; they found another way to create it.

Can you give me an example? I am kind of confused from this statement because my belief system is that if it does not work, it is not supposed to, and you move on.

Yes, and I will explain that thought to you later. Take for instance one of the biggest inventions—the airplane from the Wright brothers in Kitty Hawk. Those boys were so committed to the feeling and thought that they both knew and believed that they could create a plane that would fly, even when no one believed in them. Do you know how many people made fun of them, separated from them and even denounced their efforts?

No, I did not know that or the story.

Those boys did not give up; they kept correcting what was not working. It was as if each part of that plane had to be redone over a dozen times. How many people on your planet would do that, not being supported by their friends or family?

I get it. Not so many would do that.

Remember when you put on the conferences and you knew you *had* to do them? It took over your being.

I do. I will never forget that.

That is what they were experiencing. They had no choice. Those boys were committed even until their last breath, if that was what it would take.

So are you saying that things come from a place within us all that we must feel, breathe, know, and believe, without conditions?

Yes, that is what WE are saying. It is the vibration of the truest sense. It literally takes over your being until it is not your being.

Ok, then these great ideas or creations are not of us?

Exactly.

Hmmm.

What you will find is that when you create from a place that is beyond you, bigger than you, that is where mountains are moved, miracles take place.

William, how do you create the energy within to create that kind of commitment? And how many people are willing to do that? Some people like being simple, living comfortable lives.

Yes. What WE are saying is that some scripts are that way. Some people are just enjoying this lifetime in ways that serve their purpose. Others will fulfill their purpose of changing the world. In that process, their lives are changed as well. There are many ways of living your lives and all of them with respect are perfect and part of the tapestry of each other.

When a soul has a deep desire and a commitment to serve a purpose bigger than itself, it is already part of its journey in this lifetime or any other lifetime. When you feel that pull or tug and you just cannot shake it, your script is showing you your part. Remember, all parts are important and each part of every soul is just as important as the next.

You will create that energy within your whole being when it is time for you to show up in bigger ways. It is like a mixture of soup and those parts are already in the recipe; you will recognize them and you will taste it in all of your senses until you reflect it internally and externally.

I am starting to understand this much better. But William, how about when you try things that do not work out and sometimes it is good to move on from it?

Tammy, tell them about your friends who have lost their businesses.

In the last month, I have had three wonderful friends lose their metaphysical shops. I know two of them have been in business for over five years. The change is hard for them to go through and the relief is in letting go of all the stress and struggles for all of them. They will not have the pressure, the pushing and pulling, of trying to make it work anymore.

All three of my friends were forced to close by external conditions. I watched this unfold, and it was upsetting to see. It reminded me of my experience with the conferences. No matter how much I was committed or how many hours I worked, it did not work out the way I wanted it to. Then, to my surprise, I watched one of my friends turn her shop into a web-based online site that created more business for her with a very low overhead. It freed her up to travel and to take care of her husband.

The second owner ended up moving and meeting new friends in other states. So I am willing to see the joy that they are both living now.

So, Tammy, do you still think the results that make you happy are external? WE keep saying it did work out until it did not.

I think a mix of external and internal. I am still processing the events I produced.

It is a mix. Foremost is their own script as to what their journey is about, and second, there is a collective force on your planet that is buying into the condition of the economy and the suffering of the thought that there is not enough.

Many, many of you are going through changes right now of things that did work before and are not working now. Also, many of you have tried things and it looked like it did not work, so you changed directions. What is true for this, is that the purpose was for you to try some things even if it they did not work out. In our eyes WE see that those experiences are valuable, even if you call it a failure or mistake or extremely difficult. It was also part of your script and the only difference is that maybe you had to have more experiences of it not working out in order for it to actually work out.

Can you explain that?

It is like your friends who owned their own stores and all three of them lost their businesses. To the outside world, it looks bleak and sad and discouraging. But on our end, WE rejoiced, because the lesson was learned or the aha moment happened where they got what they needed to learn from that experience and then the play changed.

Why do some things work out in the external and some do not? My friends lost everything with their businesses and they are still trying to find themselves. These friends of mine were committed.

Tammy, with such respect for all of your experiences…yes, your friends were committed and most of the time unconditionally; however, their journeys were not supposed to be as business owners for the rest of their lives.

Your friends were supposed to own their business until they were not. It is like changing out flowers every now and then. You need to seed new flowers, new beginnings, and new ways of being. That is how you all thrive and enjoy your lives; how you meet new people, move to different places.

Are you ready to see the beauty in it all? Remember WE said you will learn from joy or pain. What that also means is that it does not matter to your soul or your psyche or your script how you get it. WE know you will get it one way or the other.

The journey will show you what you are reflecting at all times. Your outer world is your mirror and your truth to what you think and feel inside. Everyone has great opportunity to succeed and have times in his or her life where it is working and where it looks like sometimes it does not.

Your commitment will show you repeatedly what you can co-create over and over again. Everyone will have wins and losses.

Everyone will experience highs and lows. Your soul and your being have to experience the dualities of life in order to thrive and to live on your planet.

It is not always easy. Remembering the Second Principle, "What can I do now?" in every situation would help. Is that the saving grace?

Yes, you are now getting it. Keep in mind that it is just your perception about what you are going through.

I can tell you it is very hard not to judge everything as good or bad.

Tammy, tell them how you got your job at the refinery so there is better understanding why sometimes things look like they did not work out, but maybe they did in the journey.

Years ago, I was looking for another job because I blew the interview for the job I really wanted, or I thought I wanted. I put so much pressure on myself and I just blew it.

Do you think that was supposed to happen?

I guess I was supposed to blow the interview. That is hard to accept though.

Yes, it was, but you were not supposed to get that job at the probation department.

I get it. I got a job at the oil refinery, and I asked for three ways to hear about it intuitively. I heard three ways and I was holding myself back—not to judge working at an oil refinery. I did not even know what I was applying for when I went into the interview. Three men who talked to me for three hours about their lives and the oil refinery interviewed me. At one point, they asked me if I had any bad feelings about the job. I was honest enough to say that I did not know the job, so how could I have bad feelings about it? We all laughed. As soon as I walked into my house, the phone was ringing—I got the job. I was so excited and scared at the same time. This was one of the best jobs I ever had. I made more money than I had ever made and for nine years, I got to read all of the spiritual books I could get my hands on. I was employed for nine years and then was happy to move on.

Why do you think it took nine years?

Because it took me that long to learn what I needed to!

Yes it did. You read and evolved until your next job showed up to give you what you needed. WE are saying that everything is in order for your lives down to getting a job at an oil refinery. All the turns you make in your lives are set up by you in order to know yourselves. You are probably asking what would have happened if you did not take a certain job that you have worked at. What happens is another prop in the play shows up bringing similar experiences for you to work out. What you vibrate from brings experiences into your being to play out. It may require many takes—just like a movie—to work itself out until you no longer need that experience.

Yes, WE know that you can just ask, *"What can I do now?"* and it automatically takes you out of the judgment or victim energy.

That is very important to know. Thank you, William. You keep repeating this, "What can I do now?"

You're welcome. WE want to make sure you have this down in your memory so it will keep coming up for you.

When WE make decisions on the other side—and WE do even in spirit—our intention is to ask if it serves everyone's highest good. Does the ripple of the river of energy live in grace and peace? Does the feeling of harmony and hope arrive just from the thought before the action has even taken place? If it does, then WE joyfully proceed to follow through with the choice at hand. The difference between your world and our heavenly place is that there is no other choice for us. WE are given answers mostly from one hundred percent of love.

Your world will deliver you hundreds of ways to move from a choice, and most of those choices are from fear or harm and can cause hurtful experiences for you and many others. It is wise not to jump so quickly at your decisions. Having discernment and thinking things through is wise on your planet. Looking at all angles before you decide and connecting to what feels loving will release many, many experiences of pain.

William, are you saying that you are given answers mostly from a hundred percent of love?

Tammy, there are very few, but a few times now and again, WE get a choice WE know is not loving.

How can that be?

The frequencies here (without getting too complicated) are very high, but every now and then when other planets spike or release energies that are not at our level, they do spike into our vibration. It creates lower-level thinking. It is very seldom that this happens; however, I have to mention it. We are aware of this, and when that happens, WE are careful to not proceed until it wavers out of our vibration. Remember, WE are all connected: even our planets, galaxies, and the heavens. There is no separation in any way. It is like a picture that has no ending and no beginning. So, what happens on your planet affects all the other planets and the galaxies and the heavens.

This sounds like a huge responsibility. You are saying that every thought and action I do affects not just the world but other planets, galaxies and the heavens?

Yes, and that is why you are writing this book.

I get the vision of how everything is so connected.

This chapter is going to show you that you are the co-creator and have always been the co-creator. On top of that, you are the observer to your choices as well.

Your messages sound so different in this chapter. Why is that?

Because you are changing, Tammy, rising above the battlefield, and becoming more peaceful again, the suffering is ending. Everyone can do this no matter what his or her circumstances are. It is time to allow your soul's joy to surface again.

I agree. All of us want to be at peace again.

Going back to the principle, the answers come through love, intuition, guidance. Most everyone knows what intuition is, but most do not trust it. Tammy, you often say there is more fear in not listening to your intuition, and that is right. Intuition is not a gift or something only special people have. Everyone is intuitive. How you label it is not our concern. What WE pray for and see is how you listen to it and how you trust it.

You said most people do not trust it—intuition. How can you trust it?

It starts with trusting yourself again through God. Giving yourself permission to listen to your intuition and guidance and letting go of the lie that you will feel out of control if you let it in. So many people feel like that—as if they will go crazy. If you just allow yourself to listen to your intuition a few times, you will realize that it is there to support your happiness and journey. You will not want to live without it ever again.

Tammy, tell them about your extremely intuitive client who had a rough ride until you worked with her.

Ellen came to me many years ago. She is one of the most intuitive people I have ever met. As a young girl, she would get things and relay them to her mother. Ellen knew when people were going to die before they did and would tell her mother. She would know where her siblings were when her parents could not find them. Even as a small child. She was bright and very clear with her answers.

Ellen was very shocked when her mother had her put on medication to calm her intuitive abilities. The one who was the most afraid of it was her mother. To Ellen's knowledge, her grandmother had the same abilities and her mother did not want Ellen to be like her grandmother. For many years, Ellen was stifled. She joined a church that did not believe in any psychic or intuitive abilities, so the church supported her new belief that she should stuff it down and let it lay dormant.

Ellen secretly knew things but did not share them with anyone. She came to me to change that. Ellen talked to her pastor to let him know that she was working with a coach to learn more about her abilities. I was honored and excited to see how open she was. I wanted her to know that no one would hurt her, and she could use her insights for life, business, kids, family, and friends. I made sure I never brought up religion or the need to change her beliefs. I wanted Ellen to feel safe with me and to trust herself again, to move into a place that would serve her. To this day, Ellen is amazing and everyone she confides in believes in her abilities because Ellen now believes in her abilities.

You have to see what the story is that you believe in about intuition. Finding out if you can believe intuition can support you and show you easier ways in the play, or if you believe it can harm you is very important. That is the beginning of trusting yourself.

Your culture and many other cultures have a tendency to judge things that are different. Just because people use different ways and tools does not necessarily mean your way is the only way. There are many ways to plant your crops.

Can you explain that?

There are many ways to fund your venture on your planet. Simply put, the furniture you sit on everyday may not be the furniture someone else sits on. You use a couch, someone else may use a stool, someone else may use a stilt, and someone may use a pillow. What is more important to know is that no matter what people sit on, what they use feels the same way your couch does to you when you sit on it. Does that make sense to you? They get the same pleasure or pain just like you do.

Remember, Principle Two, in short, teaches you to ask what you believe in through love, then listen through intuition, guidance, and being still enough to hear it in spite of your ego.

How do you know when it is ego, intuition, or guidance?

Great question. You know when it is your intuition and guidance when you are inspired with love, joy and hope, and a sense of peace. Love feeds love, and it multiplies over and over again. Love spills out past you. You all have had experiences of that.

You will not feel any fear around it. Your intuition will present an all-knowing feeling and there will not be any presence of doubt, fear, or confusion. It may not even make sense, but you will feel it as strong and as peaceful as you can handle in your body.

If you act in confusion, fear, and doubt, you are in your ego: EGO—Exiting God's Outcome. Why would you not want God's outcome? Do you want a bumpy ride or a smooth ride? In the end, you will reach God. How you get there is up to you.

William, a lot of my clients tell me they feel like they are making things up that come to them from meditation and guidance. What should I be telling them?

This is a very common feeling. That is because the places the answers are coming from are not of your world, so any information or visions of this place will feel like you are making them up.

What you should be telling your clients and yourself is that the place you are in, in meditation or dreamtime, is real. Any time you go somewhere else besides your planet, you will feel like it is made up. What the ego part of all of you wants you to believe is that the only thing that is real is your body and the world you live in. That is how the ego will win.

Go to the place where you meditate and connect, that is the real place to be. There are unlimited realms of wisdom and knowledge you can tap into anytime. Your answers are there for all of you. Your healing's, your vast greatness, your genius energies, and your hope for your planet are there too. Your survival of your planet is also there. That is where all your great leaders tap into, too. That is how they were able to stand out from the rest. This is where great movies and music come from. They all knew where to tap into and what to use to help humankind. Your world as you are living it is not real. It is the internal part of your being that is real. I know it feels real, but it is not.

It is very common that all of you are only using 10 percent of your brains. Why use just 8 to 10 percent of your brain when you can use 12 percent? What is really interesting is that you are all moving into using 13 percent now because the veil is lifting. How do you like that? Once you pass the 10 percent of your brain cells, your intuition opens up more percentages in your brain waves. As a collective, you are all opening up more to your greatness. This is very exciting news.

I like that. What does that mean?

It means more possibilities of miracles and more possibilities of telepathy on your planet in all ways.

What do you mean in all ways?

All living energies are now capable of tapping into the Universe's wisdom. You can call it God; you can use whatever term you feel most comfortable with. The real excitement is that you will be able to tap more into each other as well.

I like that. People are less likely to hide anything from each other.

Yes. Tammy, tell them the story of how you moved to Phoenix because of a dream. Dreams also give guidance.

In 2003 I had rented a room from a friend for almost a year and really needed my own place again. I just moved back into my house and threw the last box into the trash can. I never wanted to see another box. My home was set up, and I was very happy to be home again. A few nights after that last box was thrown away, I had a dream that my Guide came to me. You know when it is a dream or a vision or guidance. It was so vivid I could not shake it.

In the dream, I was watching myself in front of a crowd doing healing work and talking to the audience. I was standing on the side with my Guide and he said to me, "As you become healed, you will be a healer and writer." I said to my Guide, "I am not a healer or writer right now." He told me again, "As you become healed you will write and heal as well." He then proceeded to tell me that if I wanted to play bigger, I had to move to Phoenix. I just looked at him without saying a word. I thought it was all crazy!

What was shocking to me is that my guide came back the next two nights to tell me the same thing, and he showed me the same dream over again. The last night I asked him, "Why you are coming back again?" He told me if he had not, I would not have followed the guidance.

So, in one month, I had to make a decision to leave everything I knew. I did not even know what I was coming to or how things were going to play out. I did have that all-knowing feeling that I had to move to Phoenix and that I would regret it if I did not. I can tell you, I was scared, but with all of my knowingness, I had to move. I did know two people in Phoenix who were very dear friends. I told them of my dream and both of them supported me and helped me immensely.

The biggest decision was moving away from my son for the first time and telling him I had to move to Phoenix because of a dream. James was supportive, but we were both sad. We had never been apart before. James was a young man now at the age of twenty-three, and I knew God would take care of him. Not only was if difficult leaving my son, but I was leaving my friends and family, too. In the comfort of my thoughts and feelings, I did have one request of God and my Guides—if I am supposed to move to Phoenix for my highest good, then my house has to sell to the first person who looks at it. To my amazement, my house sold to the first person in the first hour it was on the market. What was wonderful was that I had already been shown in a reading the house that I would buy in Phoenix. I flew to Phoenix a few times to look at houses. The second time I went, I was looking at a house and told my agent to drive around the block. To my surprise, there was the house on the corner, the same one I saw in the reading. The owners had just put the for sale sign on the front lawn that morning. My house sold and closed within three days of my moving into my new home in Phoenix.

It was the best move ever. My business grew and my friend Vickie introduced me to everyone she knew.

This story is a true example of listening and the flow of that follow-through. Everything just opened up for Tammy, and it has served her soul's journey.

The way you may download your guidance or intuition does not matter. There are numerous ways of hearing, seeing, feeling, knowing, being empathic, to receive messages. Sometimes you will receive messages or signs many times until you get it.

William, you have not mentioned meditation yet or how to listen and open up your intuition or guidance.

You must be an open channel to receive intuition and guidance. It is very easy to do that and is not as complicated as you think it is. This is another example of how the ego will work your thoughts to make you believe that it is just too hard to meditate or receive messages. Do not listen to those thoughts. Being relaxed and open is the key.

Water is such an easy way to clear energies. Take a bath, sit in the water, and ask for guidance.

Sitting outside is another way to release negative energies and allow the flow of guidance to come in.

Find what works for you and use it until you need another way. Making it harder than it is is your ego's way of not allowing your truth to come in.

Meditation is good; however, if you do this all the time, sometimes you need to change your ways of connecting. Just be open to connect. When you meditate, it feels like you are connected to everything; it is a blissful energy—a joyful connection.

You are constantly having people and other forms telling you what works. Follow through with what you are getting. Your inner voice thoughts will guide you on a clear path to answers. Trusting yourself is the first step in finding yourself.

As you learn to meditate, do not get trapped in meditating too much. WE notice that there are some people who meditate every day for hours at a time, and then feel awful when they forget. WE are saying yes, meditate—but do not let it run you. The journey of being connected to God is blending in with everyone. It is not a journey of separation and only being in certain groups. It is a journey of blending in with everyone. Give your Light everywhere you go. If you are giving your Light to a group of Lightworkers and not moving it around, then look at all of the people who are missing out on your Light as you are missing out on theirs. Meditation is a tool to feed you, to listen, to pray, to join with God, the Holy Spirit. Don't let it become an addiction. Remember you are still in a body that wants to connect to people as well.

So basically, you are saying, do not let anything run you. But sometimes we need to be around people who think the same way we do.

You do and WE recommend that you get your support, however do not let it be your end all. Let your community, friends, and churches do whatever to support you. Be open to your inner guidance to tell you what your spirit needs.

Whatever you are doing from love does not ever run you. It assists you always. Yes, you do need your support and the fellowship. Be ok if you have it or do not have it. Be neutral about it. Do not let it affect your peace if sometimes you cannot be with others.

One of the hardest things to do, especially when you are attached, is to be as neutral as possible. If you cannot be neutral, then go to someone else for help who can assist you in your answers. Your world is now filled with all kinds of healers, coaches, counselors, teachers, and pastors to assist you all. So no more excuses for being stuck. You can pay, trade, or even gift sessions with each other. One of the blessings is that your answers will keep appearing over and over again. Watch how you will get repeated messages all the time. Sometimes they are settling and sometimes they knock you over the head like a two-by-four.

One of the fears that will show up when you ask, *"What can I do now?"* is the fear of change.

Some of you will experience some moments of fear because of the unknown. WE know how frightened you all are of change. But when your life is not working, it is not working because it is not supposed to. Just like in meditation, WE told Tammy the reason her events were not successful monetarily was because if they had been, she still would be doing events. Tammy's journey is now in writing and seeing clients and learning from them as they learn from her.

If your life is not working, it is because there is another way for you to live your life. Pushing and pulling will not make it any easier.

Change is a part of you because of your planet and the vibration of the structure of your species. Be open to the beauty of change and see where that leads you. Change is a beautiful thing. Your survival mechanism is related to change. It is like water for all of you. It is a way of growing and thriving. You would wilt away if change were not part of your play. All of you would get so bored that you would will yourself to die.

I never looked at it that way. I get it. I could not be at the same job for fifty years…

Ok, seeing change as beautiful is a metaphor for life now.

Yes, it should be. William, the changes you are talking about are external and internal, right?

The true change is internal. That is the permanence of a vertical shift to your being. If you have not chosen to change internally, the Universe will help you out externally, and that can come through joy or pain. It is really all connected, because before the external part comes in, your internal was asking for it long before it happened. You can look back at your lives and see where some changes happened and you were not surprised over it because you knew it was coming; at other times, things happened that no one was expecting.

Part of Chapter Two is being still to hear. This is one of the hardest things to do at first, especially for anyone who has never done it. Once you are able to do this, you will soak it up and love your moments of hearing and being still.

Tammy, tell them about your client who could not sit still or even be alone with herself.

I had a client a few years ago who just could not sit still. It pained her to sit in my office just to talk to me for an hour. As part of this pain, she would pull in the wrong person all the time because she needed to fill that void with someone else outside of herself. My client was in so much pain that she no longer wanted her repeated cycles. On the outside, she had all the attributes: she was beautiful, smart, and easy to talk to. She could attract all the guys, but she would put a lot of pressure on those she dated to make her feel better. Every guy she was with would leave; they would break up with her because the pressure of filling her voids was too much to handle.

For homework, I had her sit for fifteen minutes a day, three days a week, without TV, radio, or phones—just with herself. I had her promise me that she would not bring anyone in for at least six months while we worked together. The first few weeks were really difficult for her, and I had a few calls from it.

By the third week, she was relaxing more around me and starting to see things differently around her. She started to enjoy herself more and was not so desperate to reach out to feel better through someone or something else. We worked together for about six months to the point where she no longer needed my services.

She is happily married now and having a baby with a man who is as healthy as she is.

This was such a gift for her to change within herself so she could change her story to a happier one.

If you have any issues or uneasiness with being with yourself, then it would be a wonderful experience for you to sit still. Make it a part of your day; three times a week is a great start.

Sitting outside in your back yard listening to the sounds of nature is a great way to feed your soul's bank account. Being comfortable in your own skin is so necessary.

To move on to Principle Three, you must create a way to be still and be comfortable with it. Because of all the electronic gadgets and the busyness, the ability to be still and listen is restricted. WE are witnessing so many people struggling with their minds, not being able to relax. Too much noise in their heads can create a huge block to hearing any kind of guidance.

Finding a way to mind dump your thoughts is a great way to relax the brain and to let go of all stored up energies that are not mindful. You can come up with many ways to release the thoughts in your head that do not serve you.

Like what?

Journal every day. Journal your thoughts and feelings and then never read them again or even judge them. Chakra clearing is the fastest way to clear not just the mind but the body's toxins. Talk to someone and release it to them. Creative arts are a great way to dump, by drawing. Working out or playing sports of any kind helps. Some people have to clean house, plant flowers, go for a walk, or go for a drive in the car.

I had a friend whose way of releasing everything was to go skydiving. She was so elated about it and I would rally her on to do it. To see how she was after her skydiving jumps was a high for her.

Whatever it takes to release, just as long it does not turn into an addiction.

William, can you tell us something inspiring.

Sure, I can tell you a story of such inspiration.

On your planet when 9/11 occurred in America, there were teams of angels assisting all of the souls coming in after they crossed over. There were so many angels and guides going to homes to help families with their grieving. It was the most inspiring gathering of love. WE were united to help all of you because, remember, your outcome is our outcome.

I do not understand why we even had to go through 9/11. Why did that happen?

Tammy, as much as there is love on your planet, there are many with hateful and disturbing thought patterns. They are just as committed to fear and wrong-mindedness as those who are committed to love and right-mindedness.

Keep committed to your right-mindedness and eventually the love will outweigh the fear and darkness. WE are counting on you all to inspire us to turn the frequencies up and to deliver us all into completeness.

This chapter is about asking every day, every moment, *What can I do now?*

William, that would be hard to do when you just lost someone—even from 9/11.

Yes, WE do understand that and there will be a time every person who lost someone even from 9/11 will ask, *What can I do now?* Or they may say, *"What Will I do now,"* because the Will is not their own.

Please explain that.

When a person asks, *"What Will I do now?"* it is the same as saying, *"Whose will should I choose now?"* God's Will or the ego's will. Asking for God's Will is the key. Asking *"What can I do now?"* is the intention of God's will, not of the ego. When your answers come to you with the feeling of peace, you will know it is of God.

I hope I am speaking for everyone reading this book. Please grace us with truth and kindness. Thank you William.

We are already doing that with all of you, every moment of the day.

So how can we lose then?

You can't lose; it just might take longer for some than others. In this book, WE are creating a shorter version of a way to truth and joy and Oneness. Are you with me?

Yes I am.

Now, coming to the part of listening to the message or response from your God Self, how do you think that happens?

By being still?

That is partly true, but not always.

Most of you hear the messages from God or the Holy Spirit or truth by just relaxing. Being still creates the ability to be at ease with your own bodies and thoughts and feelings. Finding a way to relax and unwind is one of the easiest ways to hear responses of truth that slip into your consciousness. Another way that may require you to open your intuition, so that you can hear it easier, is to go do something differently. By getting out of your own way, you're not so attached to the outcome or the play.

Remember that story on the morning show today where the musician had created the words already to a song and could not put a title to it? That was all he had left to do to the song. Do you know how long it took him to get that title?

No, I do not know him personally.

Funny, Tammy. It took him months. Because he was in a store shopping for groceries, that was the only way WE could slip him the title. It came to him from hearing someone calling out a little girls name. WE are not concerned if you get it externally or internally. WE can create props, people in the play to support you at all times.

So you were with me this morning when I was watching television?

I am one with you; I am never away from you.

Your species is finding it harder and harder to relax, to rejuvenate, or to be alone. It is becoming a crisis on your planet. Some people would judge you if you did nothing. There are so many false expectations placed on the roles you have chosen to play in your world. Do you think working non-stop and not finding time to relax is going to get what you want in the end?

There was a time I used to think that.

You now believe differently because of your own experience. You have also witnessed the story about your sister. Look at how hard she worked in this lifetime.

Yes, she did work non-stop for most of her life, and her body is showing signs of it.

Tammy, your sister has grown more spiritually and evolved more in the last three years from not working than in her last forty years of working.

Wow, that is crazy. But we have to pay the bills. So was my sister wasting her time working for those many years?

73

No, your sister got what she needed and those forty years served her. However, she could have gotten the message sooner if she wanted to. Remember, this is not a race or a reality show. It is a timeline that assists you always for the purpose of your soul's journey. It could have taken many lifetimes for your sister and that did not happen. What WE are proposing for all of you is that you will evolve at your own pace and you will reach Oneness in the end. How many years or lifetimes it takes is not our concern. What is our concern is the pain and suffering. WE do not want to see you cycle and spin into darkness, pain, and ego as often as you do. Once you release some unnecessary cycles and patterns, you will be much happier, and for that, your planet will thrive in ways WE would like to see and be witness to.

Do you want to be your house payments or be your life?

I want to be my life.

You learned that the hard way.

Just asking for another way can show you how to receive money easier without sacrificing. Doing what makes your heart sing allows you the freedom to express love to other areas of your life.

There is also a notion that you do not have time for your families. Get this—if you spent more time with your loved ones, your work would be better. You relax into a higher frequency, allowing thoughts to come in to assist you. You will not be running in circles as much.

Finding a way to relax will free you all up in your journeys. Do you remember that WE talked about feeding your soul's bank account? Find a way to feed your soul's bank account. Relaxing and giving back to yourself should be on all of your calendars. Sitting outside is one of the easiest ways.

Tammy, do you know how Gandhi relaxed?

I think I do. He would weave every day and sit outside on his compound and would have his team doing the same thing.

As he weaved, it took him out of the problems of the day and into a vibration frequency that allowed us to slip many messages to him.

Find your way. What is it you simply enjoy doing, even if it sounds silly? It is more shameful that you judge something you enjoy. Judging anything that you enjoy is your ego at its best.

Once you collectively put together all of the suggestions from this chapter, you will see and know and feel you are on your way to a healthier and happier life. Taking inventory every day to see what step you are honestly on, will shift you into the next principle if you choose it.

I do not know why anyone would choose to stay stuck, sad, or depressed.

Tammy, you would be beyond shock to know that millions and millions of souls have given up the journey to happiness, but as long as you all understand this principle, you can reawaken them to the possibilities again.

Can you imagine what a marvelous movement it would be to see the changes in everyone who reads this book and to see how it brings others to their own happiness?

I know you are thinking the responsibility is for yourself first, and that is true. Once you have restored your sanity to its rightful place in love again, you will expand that love to others without effort or hardship or without any sacrifice. You will automatically pour over to others the dreams, the hopes and the joys they have forgotten.

Your soul and the Light within you will innately relish the opportunity to share the holy Oneness of all of us.

Part of the purpose of your soul's bank account is to share. If it does not have anything to share, it looks for other people's energy to fill it up. Many, many people are going around taking energy from others, and it is a cycle that is getting worse on your planet. It is affecting your children and your animals. They are the easiest targets to take from, and they most easily fill up their own bank accounts. Learning to relax will rejuvenate not just yourself but also your children and your animals. WE can see that the energies are being replaced to overflowing again and are no longer deficient.

The countries WE really enjoy watching are Finland, France, Austria, Israel, Lithuania and Morocco. In these countries, they give more time off as a promotion to their workers. WE see their cultures giving an average of forty paid days off a year including holidays. That is a well-defined example of how to relax. WE also want to mention that it comes off as a luxury to others that they get more time off to enjoy life. Most of your nation is about making the money, grinding, and working long hours to make more to spend. How is that working for all of you? It is not even a balancing act. It is an inventory to see what is working in your lives and what is not working.

Understanding your part in the play and your responsibility on this planet can shift all of your perceptions. The person you are waiting on to show up is yourself. The ego would have you believe that once you get that job, car, body, house, money, etc., then you will be happier and be willing to show up. That will never happen that way. Once you get *you* to show up… the car, house, money, body will show up. You can only SHOW up when you start helping others at winning. Also, affirming that *you* are winning helps as well.

Again, ask, *"What can I do now?"* It shifts you into taking responsibility for being the one creating your life and your outcomes, good or bad. Responsibility is a vital part in your makeup as a person and soul. Taking responsibility shifts everything. How many people on your planet do you know who do not take responsibility for their own actions? The numbers are very high, and most of that is due to souls that are not evolved yet, not awake yet, or do not want to wake up in this lifetime.

What do you think happens to those who do not wake up? Yes, they die. They cannot survive on your planet without taking responsibility. Many of the souls who do not take responsibility turn into addicts, or worse, they go into victim energy that takes them to such low points, they take their own lives or will themselves to die.

William, this sounds so drastic.

It is drastic. How many mothers and fathers have lost children from suicide? How many souls have been so self-destructive because they did not feel they had any choices? They could not get the perception that maybe there was another way. Many parents have come to you with help after their child committed suicide.

I understand. It is not just about me moving forward.

Yes, all of you taking responsibility to move forward and to change with the principles at hand are now helping those around you, just from your vibration. Your hope, your joy, your journey alone can change a life.

Take this seriously: without the change on a collective front, from this day forward, your planet will not survive in a joyful way. There is much hope available from us for you, and you have the tools and means to change yourself, your neighbors, your community, your cities, your state, your countries, and then your world. It starts like a festival of Light that has no ending to touch everyone and everything it comes in contact with. How strong to do think your Light is and how committed are you to your change and your Divine outcome? WE promise a happy ending, as long as you remember your Oneness, your Light and your purpose.

Can you conceive on any level within your soul how many people can be influenced by your Light, your choices, your thoughts and your feelings? If you knew that others depended on you finding your way so that they could find their way, would that make a difference? Would that influence your decision to play bigger? Would you be willing to shine your Light no matter what?

I think you are getting the seriousness of our conversations here that you matter more than you know. Your influence is felt, heard, and seen by those around you. Your choices affect everyone, and how you show up is how WE all show up. The ripple keeps rippling and the tides of all of your souls can deliver us from such depths of the darkness to the Light.

You all have done wonders in your lifetimes. WE are saying on behalf of the universes, the galaxies, and the planets that you matter more than your Lights, your souls, and your thoughts. You are miracles walking in bodies to abolish the fears and the separateness you believe in. Let go of the separateness and the pain. Now take responsibility to change, allowing the Divine essence of God to flow through you.

Going on to Principle Three. Are you ready?

YES!

The 3rd Principle:
BECOME THE RECEIVER OF GRACE & GUIDANCE

Know that you are worthy to receive the help and guidance that you are seeking and treat yourself accordingly.

Now that you are in Chapter Three, you are starting to see the cycles better and the patterns you buy into. This is such a relief for all of you. It is symbolic as if you are taking off a weighted coat that you have been wearing for decades. You are now letting go of some of your unnecessary distractions. WE are watching all of you as you are releasing the fears and the hurts and the illusions your world is accustomed to.

Becoming the receiver of grace and guidance is also a new way of receiving energy in the form of love. This may be new for most of you, and for those who sometimes do allow themselves to receive, they will learn how to receive more often.

Having self-worth is the mix you are made of, meaning it's already a part of you. It is the fundamental key to any success in your life. It can make you or break you. So what do you think self-esteem is?

I believe self-esteem is a part of your deep-rooted beliefs that you have for yourself. It is the good and the bad that make up what we hold true for ourselves. It is what you think and feel about yourself.

That is partially true. What is true about self-esteem, self-worth, is that it is always changing on top of what you have already ingrained into your psyche. It is those hidden thoughts you bury very deeply. Sometimes those thoughts stay buried for many lifetimes without you digging them up. Once you are willing to start bringing up your feelings and distinguish the truth, you will define your self worth differently. You will do this because the pain will become unbearable or maybe even through revelations, or miracles. Maybe in your lifetime you will have a yearning in your soul to know your Higher Self better.

Ok, so how do you recover those thoughts? Do we all have these thoughts?

Yes, you all have those thoughts. Your experiences create those thoughts—good or bad—and you store them away. Some of those thoughts and feelings serve you and others harm you. To recover those thoughts is to be really open to look at some of your experiences and ask why this or that experience has not worked out for you. And why has that other experience worked out? What do you believe with that thought? What thoughts and feelings do you harbor as you go through painful experiences? What are you settling for?

Here is another question that you should be asking. *Why does it appear that some people have everything they want?* If you are not operating from that vibration, then maybe it is because you feel you do not deserve it on some level. Your patterns and experiences have shown you that you fall under the radar more times than not.

Ok, what do you think some of the traits are for insecure people—from your own experiences?

Hmmm. I think insecure people doubt themselves. They do not trust their own answers. They are always looking for someone else to make them feel better. They take things very personally. They are very conditional with themselves. Insecure people will not try to do anything new unless they have to. Most insecure people will play it very safe in order to shield themselves from chances of happiness because they are afraid they might mess up, and they cannot handle failure. They live in the victim energy and are negative, not hopeful, about life. Some live in the past or the future.

Yes, this is a great start in looking at some of the behavior of insecure people. The reason WE are bringing this up is so that you have no doubt about what an insecure person looks like. WE are here, so please allow yourself to go at your own pace to see some of the illusions that do not serve you anymore.

Insecure people are those who cannot take responsibility for their own mistakes and choices in life. They will project and blame others and never think they are responsible. The thought that they created any hardship would be too much to take on. They are always waiting for the other shoe to drop, seeing the glass half empty.

That sounds like someone who is not awake or aware.

Yes, it does, and that can be a part of their makeup They are not ready. There are very secure people on your planet who are not awake, do not even believe in God, and are very successful. (We will talk about being awake and aware in Chapter Ten.) Most insecure people will punish themselves before they look past themselves.

What?

Insecure people will take the blame for something that has gone wrong and will not hold anyone accountable. They take the brunt of the pain. They compound many wounds on top of each other. They will see all love as conditional, because the love they have for themselves is conditional. Another quality of insecure people is that they are rarely flexible with life. It is much safer for them to play out the same day over and over as much as possible. Eventually this will cause more unhappiness. They do not see themselves as an equal to anyone else and will not question anyone, even if it is questionable. They pull back and do not feel like they are a part of the play. Most insecure people are not happy and isolate themselves.

You are saying most insecure people will take the blame for something and will not hold someone else accountable, even if it is not their fault? My belief system from the Course is that there are no victims.

Yes, that is true; however, through pain or joy you will learn and grow soulfully. No one is a victim of any experience.

But, William, you did say some insecure people also project and will not take responsibility for their actions, right?

81

Yes, I did. That is because on the one extreme they put all the blame on others. Insecure people will vacillate to both extremes, to either taking all of the blame or not owning any of the blame.

Can you give an example? This sounds like all illusions of fear.

Sure. An insecure person who blames others is also a person who some call a bully in school. These kids are so insecure, they deliberately attack other kids in school for no reason. Then they have false stories in their heads about why they attacked another kid or teacher. Some kids grow out of this when they start to own their issues. Some do not. However, finding out the truth about this trait is allowing the healing to take place. The ability to see some of your beliefs can release future painful experiences.

Ok, William, I give. How do we do this?

It is very simple. What traits do you like about yourself and how have they served you in this lifetime? Take inventory of your qualities that work because you want to keep those and recognize their value. Second, make a list of those traits that you do not like about yourself, **without judging them.** Ask God or the Holy Spirit how you can change those traits. One of the most effective ways is to take small steps toward change.

Can you give an example, please? Because talking about self-esteem is so basic, I would think we all know about self-esteem.

Do you really think that from working with all of the clients you have and your own issues with self-esteem that you really understand what self-esteem is? Do you think those clients came to you because it was just their own issues?

No, I am humbled. I get it.

Ok, for example, you may say: *I am not always responsible. I cannot work or hold down a job.* You can look at this two ways. How does not working serve me and how does it not serve me? What are the consequences from not being responsible? Have I been this way my whole life? Has it hurt anyone in any way? When did this trait start in my life?

Say you did not want to work, and your number one priority was to always have someone work for you or take care of you. Now remember this is not always hurtful unless you settle for someone or something to support your belief that sacrifices your truth and pulls you away from love. You can see the type of people you bring into your life who may or may not be for your highest good. If you feel and believe that not being responsible is okay, look at your life.

Tammy, tell them about your clients from many years ago—the married man who needed his wife to work for the first time because he lost his job.

Before I go into this story, William, I am not sure she was not being responsible. Maybe the fear of working was because it was a major change for her.

Remember, not all traits of insecurity are one hundred percent, but if the cycle keeps appearing, your beliefs need to be shifted. Remember that there may be more than one belief or story that plays into wrong thinking. Knowing this story, this is a trait Sue carried with her since she was a child.

Ok, I met Larry and his wife Sue years ago, and what a wonderful couple they were. Larry and Sue were on a mission to find their spiritual path. Larry lost his job and was floating from job to job. His wife Sue had not worked since they married over twenty years ago. Sue was a stay-at-home wife.

When I met both of them, they were in trouble financially and Larry could not carry them anymore with his side jobs. He asked Sue if she could just get a part-time job to supplement their income for a few years until they recovered. Sue was frantic about even looking for a job and was very hesitant. Sue was not lazy, but she was extremely afraid to open any doors to working.

Larry started to put pressure on her, and by that weekend, Sue fell down a flight of stairs and broke her right arm in many places, as well as her collar bone. The doctors said it would take up to two years for her to recover fully. The doctors wanted to schedule many operations to try to repair the damage. It was obvious to me what she had done. It was easier for her to have physical pain and repair work on her body than to get a job. Sue had less fear about hurting herself than getting a job to help out.

What does this have to do with self-esteem?

If you can just look past the change Sue had to make to help out financially, then you would see that maybe she felt insecure about working. Maybe she believed she could not do a job or was not good enough.

This is just a story that has an example of someone with self-worth issues. Now let's take this another way. What does a person look like who has healthy self-esteem, self-worth?

Easy, they will do whatever they believe in and follow through without worry about what others think of them. They possess self-confidence and hold their head high. They believe in their dreams and are very positive people. They take chances when necessary, and they have active lives. They are co-creators of their journeys. Most secure people are flexible and can handle many things at once. They speak up for themselves and won't allow someone to take advantage of them. They do not take anything personally. Secure people honor themselves. They honor their feelings and obligations, relationships, life. They know their value, their inner value, their influence on themselves and the world. They have self-respect and a commitment to take care of themselves and their daily activities.

Yes, so see the difference. For the most part, the people on your planet are in the middle of this. There may be some issues that bring up insecurities, and other issues do not bother them at all. Some people get insecure around family members. Some people get insecure about their bodies, jobs, love relationships. The list goes on and on.

Many insecurities can come from not understanding how to play out a part that shows up in your play. Say someone asked you to ride a horse around the corral. How would you feel about that?

Scared and not very secure.

If you had that show up in your play, what would you do?

I would read up all about it and maybe go take some lessons first.

Then would you feel more secure?

Yes, I would.

Imagine that two candidates showed up for the same interview. Let's just say they were the same age and had the same education and employment background. Let's say one of the two candidates was not feeling very secure about doing the interview. The other was confident, expecting to get the job. Who do you think got the job?

Easy—the confident one.

Do you think that candidate could do a better job than the other?

I don't know.

Apply that scenario to your client Jill who had the same interview that Dan had. Both candidates were qualified, but because Jill was insecure, Dan got the job. In reality, Jill would have done a better job. Because she forgot her greatness and had some moments of not believing in herself, she lost that job.

I get this, William, however, maybe she was not supposed to get that job she interviewed for—like you talked about in Chapter One.

Tammy, yes, she was not supposed to get that job, and unless she is willing to see her greatness, she may have many interviews before she understands how valuable she is. One day she will show up in her greatness and get the job. Confidence and self-esteem are internal traits that show externally. You can never hide how you feel inside. Every aspect of your life reflects that. It is all energy. By talking about all the traits of your humanness, you will come to an understanding of how much you operate from your unloving aspects. WE are hopeful you will strip away the barriers and struggles. Just by looking at this collectively, there is new hope for your planet. You will take after take, until you know and believe this in the deepest part of your soul that you are love, encased by a body that cannot contain what is so expansive and Godly.

Just imagine someone who was instructed to hit a wall with his body over and over again. How many takes will it take before he says, *I cannot do this anymore. Is there another way to play this part out?* That is what you are looking for. You all get so attached to the props in the play, you have forgotten that you are the one who matters the most. The inner changes are what causes the props to show up. How are your props showing up?

Another example of people allowing low self-esteem to come in is when they are going through a difficult time. Most of the time your hard times pass and you move out of them. Recognizing that all illusions arise from your hard times. Windows of opportunity will bear witness to your thinking is from—love or fear. The ego part of you will try to convince you that your happiness depends on what you have or what is fading out. This causes such distress. Can you be open to the possibility of knowing and believing in your greatness, your worth, your soul, your heart—that you are a great and divinely magnificent being? The evolution of your species is God's work. How can you not be great?

Tammy, tell them the story about Elizabeth, who knew her greatness before others recognized it with her.

I forgot about this. Elizabeth came to me many years ago. She was very intuitive and believed in all of her heart she wanted to be a singer. That is what truly made her happy. She had a great job at the time, but it did not feed her soul's bank account and it drained her. When I started to coach her, she decided to quit her job and to get gigs for singing. The belief that she knew she would make it was there. All she needed was a plan and to follow through with it.

Elizabeth had so many people judging her for her choice to stop working. Most of the reactions were from others who could not believe she was following her dreams. They did not believe in their dreams either. They didn't think that she was being responsible. It was a joy for me to witness. Elizabeth was elated and happy to change and to create her journey. She started her business and was very smart to open doors to find gigs. It was not an easy decision because she ended up moving home to her family, but that is when the doors started to open for her. I know she is singing now around the Texas region and is working at a television show. She also found the love of her life in Texas.

Take into account that Elizabeth had some struggles, but she knew deep in her soul that her music was her salvation. Other doors opened up for her that supported her dream. Tell them how you were affected by this.

I felt encouraged to continue to follow my desires to do the events. The experience of knowing and working with Elizabeth was so inspiring and rewarding to witness. I saw myself in her and watched her swing from fear to love until it leveled out.

Tammy, she is you...You were experiencing the same journey with different props.

I love it. Thanks for that, William.

This is very important to know—once you have a sense of worth for yourself, you will begin to TRUST your guidance and your intuition. TRUST releases the blocks that stop you from receiving guidance. TRUST—Taking Responsibility Uniting Souls Together. WE know that from your journeys, you will take more responsibility without any judgments.

Let's talk about grace. What do you think grace is all about?

Having favor with someone or God. In the dictionary it says "to have a pardon or favor."

Yes, one way of saying—the God way of saying—you have grace is to say your request has been recognized. Your dilemma has been solved and resolved. Your vibration is in the frequency for you to reach for your soul's solution. Your question has been answered. Do you know what soul stands for?

Do tell. I have no clue.

SOUL—Standing Out Under Layers. This means that in spite of your layer of fears, your soul is standing out to expose the love of divine intelligence. You are all standing out under layers of fear to expose the truth of love and the rebirth of your innocence, your brilliance. God is expressing through you, and your souls are the engines that create your experiences.

Grace is part of the key to your soul's engine because the spark of grace releases all favor to all of you. Every one of you possesses this ability. You are all granted a clemency, a permanent immunity, to get all of your free passes of grace. Grace is unlimited to all of you at all times, day or night, any hour, any minute, or second of the day.

WE are eager to share in your grace—your allowance of grace and guidance. WE rejoice in your victories and your celebrations. WE share in your moments of sadness as well. Grace comes when you are open and honest to say you are ready for help, when you know you are worth receiving the help and direction from a power greater than yourself.

Sounds so wonderful. (Just sighing). A powerful message, William, of divine Light and love.

Yes, a powerful message that is a part of you, a part that is reflected also from God.

Remember that all of you are pleasing to God, your guides, and the angels. Can you now open up to pleasing yourself?

Grace is for everyone. No one is excluded. For sure, no one is special yet everyone is special always.

Can you please give an example of grace?

Sure, do you know the story of Nelson Mandela?

Some of the story.

Here is a very brave soul on your planet who lived a very difficult life in his earlier years. He was imprisoned for being an anti-apartheid activist. Nelson was sentenced to prison for the rest of his life. He served twenty-seven years and still came out to make a difference.

Grace came to him through his own origin and the prayers of his followers. Nelson Mandela is a pure example of grace and guidance. His life changed drastically and he was given a Nobel Peace Prize. After he was released, Nelson became the president of Africa for six years. If Nelson Mandela can be open to grace, so can you. This is a hero and a leader who went from the depths of darkness to the light of dawn. Do you believe he thought his glass was half empty? To most peoples' surprise, he did not think so.

What an inspiring story. It is really amazing how his journey took him through the darkest of times to the lightest of times.

Do you think Nelson Mandela only saw Light when he was released from prison?

He had many wonderful moments in prison that were delightful, and he was connected to the divine energy of love. The props were not his condition for happiness. Yes, there were moments of hardship, mostly because he missed his family and their time together. He missed the connections he had on the outside. Do not be fooled by the props that display your madness or support your happiness. Your true happiness is woven deep within your souls, your beingness. Even your darkness and ego parts are woven deep in your souls and beingness. Now is the time to resurrect the dark and transmute it into the Light so you can discover your innocence once again. There are many on your planet who have the most beautiful props and people in their lives, yet they are miserable because they are not connected to their inner selves. They are not healed completely.

You can call it grace or guidance, whatever you like. It would be very serving to you to use it. WE are always waiting to be used and of service to all of you. You automatically run in circles until you realize your answers are within you already.

As you read in the sub-heading of this chapter, it says "Know that you are worthy to receive HELP." Excuse the limited wording with our conversation, but allowing yourself to receive help is a key to opening the door for God's hand to rescue you.

HELP—Heavens Erasing Legitimate Problems. Be open to the thought that maybe you can help yourself by handing anything that needs to be solved over to God/Holy Spirit. It is a choice to ask for help. You want to become the receiver of grace and guidance.

On your planet, you will not make it very easily on your own. Just admitting that you are open to grace and guidance will relieve much pain in your life.

The ego will be very clever to say that you are so weak to ask for help from anyone or God. The ego is going to create whatever story it can to hold you back to denounce your greatness and your connection to Source energy. It is like having a telephone line already cabled into yourself that you do not use very much. You can tap into this line anytime for help. This is your true phone line to call 911 and 411 when you need it. Being comical about it, you have your own operator at all times and WE do not charge you for it. You have your own personal service twenty-four hours a day, and most of you do not use it very much. Just for the fun of it, you can create your own phone and use it to talk to your belief system or your Higher Self. Start somewhere. I know what you are thinking. You are thinking that sounds so crazy. Who and what do you think babies are talking to when they play with toy phones?

I do not know.

Most of the time they are talking to us, God, angels, or people who are on the other side. WE hear their messages just like yours, even if they are not talking in words. There are many ways to talk to us.

Like what?

Some people do prayers in silent words. These prayers are feelings and the call for help is in that. All the energy of requests for help comes in many forms of communication. WE are open to all forms. It is the intention that opens the channels so WE can hear your requests and help.

Some requests come through cries, feelings, thoughts, words, singing, drumming, or driving in your cars. WE pick up your request. Some are from your meditations, group prayers, your synagogues, churches, homes. Some requests come from dreamtime where instant healings can and will take place. Others come from your past or future lives that are lining you up on your journeys. Some of your prayers for help come from your ancestors and your family members or others who do not even know you.

How can our past or future lives help us? How can members of our families or people we do not know intervene to help us? How can our ancestors help us?

Tammy, all souls are derived from a frequency that expands, and it is inter-dimensional to who you are. You are more than this one experience on planet Earth and because of that, you vibrate all of your past and future lives. You are all living the past and future at the same time. Now, if you can understand this, then believe that parts of your future and your past lives are healing you right now. As you heal one aspect of your life, it vibrates and changes the rest of your lives. Remember, love heals and expands. Because there is no separation, family members, or people you do not know can be healing you by the intention to see you healed already. When the intention for you comes from unconditional love, no matter who holds it, it is the miracle of help. The form of the illusion is abolished and rebuked by the mere request. Another miracle happens when you request a healing or help for others, you also receive a healing. It is quite beautiful to witness.

Watching all of you, WE see that some of you are more open and connected, meaning that you are living in a relationship with God or your Source. Because of a devotion or practice that many have on your planet, they already have their phone line in service and use it to help others. Even when you pray for family members, or people you do not even know, you are creating a vortex of unconditional love that lifts everyone higher from where they were vibrating, including yourself. Consider what you are experiencing with Egypt. Many around the world are praying for the highest good of everyone and order from chaos. Your prayers are being answered.

I now get the deepness to our prayers. We need to begin praying more. Are our intentions also a form of prayer?

Yes, all of your intentions, along with your affirmations, are a form of request. Prayer works, and many other ways work as well.

Your ancestors are also helping all of you. Those souls who have not incarnated and are somewhere else are praying for you. Do you know that many other planets you do not know of are also praying for Earth to heal and to rise above the fear levels you all stay in?

Those planets know that your frequencies affect theirs. As you pray for the Earth, you may want to include all planets of the Universe. Also, know that praying for just your country is limited. Pray for all your countries. Pray for your planet.

When WE pray for your planet, WE send love and energy to your planet as a whole. WE can intervene to help individuals as well as cities, states, and countries when needed. What happens in most cases if you are not feeling worthy or do not believe in the help, the energies of the help bounce off of you and do not hold to change the situations you get into. Now, it is not every time that it bounces off. Sometimes it stays and penetrates your beingness so that miracles can take place. But those who know they are worthy and are open to receiving help bring in many miracles. They are witness to the results and make it a daily practice to receive help. Experience is wisdom, and the more you receive help from something greater than you, the more you will expand your consciousness into vibrations you are not even aware of yet. When you expand, you expand everyone else. As you rise, you raise everyone as well. You collectively move forward or you can move backwards from your thoughts.

William, I am moved on the deepest level of knowing and really getting to understand how we are all so connected—that there really is no separation.

Yes, and that is the thrill of it all. WE are talking about how you are so connected as beings, but you are also so connected to the animals and the plants and the Earth and the stars and the moon and the galaxies of the Universe. You are connected to us and the angels. As you are connected to the angels, you are also connected to the Light and the dark. You have the choice to be connected to any level of Light or dark. It is up to you. As you think it, you will create it. As you live it, you will experience it.

Your decisions and choices affect everything, small or large. Your thoughts throughout the day affect your plants, your animals and the air you breathe on your planet. Do you think that the air in the larger cities is just smog and toxins? No, it is not. It also made up of particles of thoughts and changes from your own frequencies. What you think and feel affects everything—not just living things, but tangible and intangible things.

How do you feel about that?

It is mind-boggling. So, when I look at a mountaintop, it affects that mountaintop?

Yes, you are now getting it. What thoughts do you think about that mountaintop when you are looking at it? Are you sending love and appreciation for it or judging it? The Course in Miracles says, *you cannot lose what you value.* If you value it, it stays. If you do not value it, it will go away. Sending loving thoughts to all things you see that bring you joy changes and frees the heavier frequencies. What you appreciate in that mountaintop or person is what you are appreciating in yourself too. You are connected to everything and everyone your eyes can see in front of you as well as what you cannot see.

Now, WE are moving on in the sub-heading of Principle Three to the word *seeking*. WE are breaking down the sub-heading so that you will totally understand what it means as you live this principle. WE want to eliminate the opportunity for confusion or misunderstandings.

What do you think *seeking* means?

To try to find the answer or to search for something?

The term *seeking* as used in the sub-heading means two things. When you are open to seeking, you own the fact that you do not have the answer yet. You are aware and open to the possibility that what you are searching for has not yet arrived. This is an important moment for all of you. The second aspect of the word *seeking* means you are now allowing God/angels/your Source to help you. You are now putting energy into opening up vibrationally for your phone line to receive grace and guidance. You are honoring your place in your play that is requesting service above and beyond yourself.

This is where the miracle is taking hold of you and changing your outcomes to grace. You are seeking relinquishment from your own nightmare, freedom from your own doing, freedom from wrong thinking, and freedom from being a victim rather than a co-creator.

Seeking is delivering you from yourself to your Higher Self. You are creating conviction when you are seeking. You know that this is your salvation and your chance to regain love and harmony in your life. When you are seeking, it is a beautiful time for you all because you are changing the play to a happier and healthier outcome.

Tammy, tell them the story about how you were seeking in your early thirties.

I remember that I felt lost and I had more questions than answers to life. I had made many mistakes in my life, and I wanted to know God and what was the truth about why we were all here. I could not believe we were just our house payments.

Why do you believe you felt compelled to seek?

I knew I did not have the answers I needed, and I wanted to feel better about living my life. I knew deep down I had been very lost and wanted to live another way. I was not fulfilled inside and wanted the connection and the answers.

Yes, and what did that do for you?

It took me into many years of seeking and searching and experiencing God, because I had not felt it since I was a child. I read everything I could get my hands on and took classes and workshops and learned to meditate. I pulled away from God to only find God again. It was like an undoing of what was not Godly and I became child-like again.

Now, has seeking and searching all of those years changed you?

Yes, I am not the same person. I changed drastically and I am still seeking.

That is what WE want all of you to do—challenge yourself to seek every day. It can take minutes to moments to days to years and life times to change. Seeking is a soulful journey that becomes rich and rewarding and divine. It is your lifeline, your juice to your soul's bank account. It gives deep reverence to your journey. Seeking gives meaning to your life. Seeking can define your essence and bring clarity to confusion. Seeking is opening the faucet to nourish yourself. It is the food that can feed you. Seeking is your Light turned on again.

When you are seeking, it allows the answers to arrive quicker for you. This also is a time when you may be given answers to make external or internal changes in your life. The answers that come with seeking are divine and driven from love and wisdom. You are being re-calibrated back into your greater Self.

You will know that you are changing. You will feel it within your being. Things will feel differently and you will have more peace of mind. You will start to think differently and will let go of more the lower frequencies that have been plaguing you for so long. You will deliver yourself from small-mindedness and petty thinking.

Getting to the last part of the sub-heading is to know that you are worthy of receiving and to treat yourself accordingly. This is the opportunity to take steps to move forward. This is sometimes the time to change directions or to end or start new things in your life.

Seeking is also a time of a strong connection to Source and your intuition, so you will be hyper-sensitive to answers, and you will know what to do for sure. Honoring yourself and "treating yourself accordingly" is to follow through with your guidance. You all know the truth of what to do and not do. It is time to step up to the plate and to love yourself enough to follow through with the answers you are getting.

One thing WE want to tell you is that if you are still questioning what to do and the answers you have gotten, go get validation from someone. Truth always repeats itself. You will hear the answers from other sources until you can own it yourself.

How do we do that? How can we get repeated messages?

Just ask for repeated messages for your highest good. Ask even for the right people to come in or a song or a saying on a TV show to confirm your answers. There are many vehicles WE can tap into to give you your answers. Do you know how worthy you are to be happy and whole? Do you know sacrificing love because you are afraid of change is fear-based?

You would not be reading this book if you did not want to be happy and healed. You are now recovering from darkness. You are receiving the Light and the resurrection of life. Your soul brought you to this book to live life with passion and a desire to change everyone back to One again.

Your life matters to others as much as to yourself. Are you affecting the world from love or from fear? Are your memories of the past serving you and others or are they bring up hardship and pain?

"Treating yourself accordingly" is a time capsule that has landed on your steps to propel you into your journey's work. It is a flicker of time undoing the past and releasing the future completely with unwavering faith. This creates the moments you are in now to receive and give miracles.

Everything you do is from a frequency of love or fear, so questioning your actions to see if you are making your decisions from love or fear is liberating. You will see most of your past choices were from fear. Now moving forward, you will observe and treat all of your choices with love and watch how your life calms down. The peace will be present for you to experience.

Take heed in knowing you may experience some fear of doing something new. Honor that fear, but do not give it any credence or thought. Your ability to aspire direction that is loving creates direction that is loving. WE are here for you always and applaud your bravery for truth on your journeys.

Keeping up with your beliefs and allowing yourself to receive guidance, knowing you are worthy of the answers, is a major victory. This is how you will move into your service, your calling, your purpose.

"Treating yourself accordingly" also is a time to be kind to yourself—to be your own best friend. It is a time to acknowledge that you are regaining your stride. Let go of the blame and guilt and know you are in repair mode. WE must acknowledge that you are already great, but you forgot that. So when WE refer to your repairing or healing, you are only healing and aligning your thoughts back to the original form of thought of who you are. You are Gods of Light. You are not broken or damaged goods, your goods are pure and innocent. You have shaded them with lies that are not of your true nature. As WE hold our thoughts to yours, the solutions to regaining who you are and will be eternally is take off the layers of illusions. It is like taking off a dirty jacket. Can you imagine how great that would feel? Some of you may have five to twenty dirty jackets on at once. That is why when you allow the help from something greater than you, you automatically feel better.

Why do you think WE ask you to play Janet Jackson's song *Velvet Rope* over and over again while you are writing this chapter?

I do not know. I just know the thoughts and the words make me cry. We have a special need to feel that we belong. I feel a strong conviction to do better.

Tammy, the reason this song is felt so deep inside you is that WE are feeling the words with you and the words are truth. The conviction that Janet puts into singing these words is also another type of prayer in the form of a song. This is how WE are reaching out to everyone in many forms to touch the depths of your souls, to rekindle the likeness of Light, so that you can thrive in ways you have not yet. How much suffering do you really need? Again your planet is begging you all to remember.

Many of your artists are channeling forms of love and Light in their works that are given to all of you to experience. WE are constantly striving to show you ways to remember your greatness.

So many energies of the likeness of God are flowing thousands of ways all over your planet, to show you in glimpses how to look and feel beyond your bodies and to witness the beauty of life and transparency of time and space. Are you with us, joined with us to change your futures? WE pray that you will want another outcome, rather than the ego's outcome. WE are expressing through all of you the desires to serve above and beyond your current day-to-day choices. What is it going to take for you to remember who you really are? Do you really think you are just a body?

Collectively on your planet, what do you think it looks like?

I believe collectively it probably looks really Light and really dark. I remember I had a dream that the planet was half dark and half Light. I could not sleep because I thought I was not doing enough.

Yes, Tammy, that is a true dream you had over ten years ago. But what do you think it looks like now?

Not sure.

Your planet is about fifty-two to fifty-six percent darkness, and it sways in that energy. Your Light goes from about forty-eight to fifty-two percent. Much work is needed to literally lighten up your planet. Your thoughts affect the planet. You make up the percentages of your dark and your Light. The history of the constitution of your species shows that the percentages of Light and darkness stay in these percentages even as more souls are incarnated. WE are requesting and holding the thought and belief that you can increase the Light NOW. Are you motivated yet to stand tall, to allow us to work through you?

WE honor that the Light is stronger than the darkness, but if you believe in the illusions more than you believe in the truth of who you are, it holds everyone in darkness.

WE are constantly reminding you of your greatness because you have forgotten. Repeat messages are necessary so that just maybe you will get the conviction, the desire, to stand up for what you need to do to express love through you. Love comes through you not from you. Letting the Light and love filter through you does not destroy you or take anything from you. Love never tires you; it never hurts you. It liberates you and everyone around you.

Martin Luther King's life was another brilliant story of one soul on your planet who strived for greatness and really understood that we are all one—we all have equal rights. Most of you know his story, but did you know that he knew on a soul level it could take his life to make a stand for equal rights? What Martin Luther King showed was a deep conviction for change that needed to happen on your planet. He changed the world by his dedication that still inspires everyone. If you are thinking that one soul cannot make a difference, then think again. That small thinking is a LIE —Living In Ego.

Tammy, why do you think you ran into Yolanda King many years ago?

What?

Why do you think that happened?

Her message was inspiring. I felt like I was not moving forward, afraid to take any chances.

Yes, but there is more to it than that. You were given a glimpse of the energy of what is possible. Yolanda knew that standing up for the truth set her free, and she had a calling to share that with everyone. You ended up moving to Phoenix and doing the conferences to do the same. It is just like when you met Maya Angelou's mother when you were in college. What did that do for you?

I was in my twenties, and when Maya's mother walked into the room, it took my breath away. It was the first time I was in the presence of someone who owned her power, her essence. I could not understand it, but I loved it. I started to think maybe I could start honoring myself more. She checked on me often to inspire me to believe in myself. It was a time I will never forget.

Yes, all people have many others come into their lives to show them what is possible. All of you have had many encounters with wonderful souls who are showing you your own greatness. Just because they are living their greatness does not mean you cannot live yours.

Your experience on Earth is a dream you all wanted to dream. You all had the ability before you incarnated to know that you could rise above the fears your world believes in. But once you incarnated, you have all experienced the duality of Light and dark. Now is the time to choose the Light over the darkness. You could challenge us to say that the Light is more powerful than the darkness, and WE agree; however, you are all allowing the darkness in. Why is that? Why is it that your world is still in the belief system that you need to take care of yourself over everyone else? That greed is high on the list of casualties of your planet....Holding on to the thought that you will win at any cost costs everyone dearly, and it will come back to plague you all. WE know this sounds serious because it is. WE still hold strong beliefs of love and a joyful outcome. Recognizing the flaws and the illusions gives the power back to you and shows you what is possible.

Principle Three is so celebratory because you are now owning that you cannot do it on your own anymore. WE jump for joy as WE see the possibilities lining up for you.

Are you now worked up to move on to Principle Four?

I do believe we are all ready to move on to Chapter Four. I am feeling many feelings right now and am ready to do whatever is necessary to serve God.

That is what WE are requesting. Thank you all.

The 4ᵗʰ Principle:
FAITH WITH NO HESITATION

Learn to release your fears so that you can accept guidance.

Now WE are moving along very nicely with the principles, and you will be aware that your life should be becoming much easier for you. You have symbolically laid down your fight- or-flight patterns. Your true essence is starting to poke its head out, so to speak. You are now taking a huge breath and you are believing that there is another way of living and experiencing your life. (*Sighing*) You are realizing on a deep level that you have choices and that you can trust and have faith in something greater than yourself.

This is a joyous occasion, because you are now owning your God-given power that is inside of you. This is how the pilot light is lit to burn a desire to serve a better purpose for your Self. You are trusting again. You are believing in you as well. You have cleared the way for the Light to shine again. You have purified your spirit for recognition of the resurrection. You no longer are nailed to the cross and are starting to stand again. You are getting off your knees.

William, I have to go back to this—what if someone does not believe in God? What would he or she be believing in then?

Tammy, the semantics are not important. If people do not believe in God, then that is their choice. What is important is that they start to believe in themselves again. Some people believe in the Earth as their master. Some believe in Buddhism, some people believe in the ancestors, or native Indian traditions. Some people believe in things you are not even aware of. It does not matter what you call your Gods, masters or even if you do not believe in God. What is crucial is the inner belief in Self—the ability to treasure you, to take ownership in yourself. This means to have merit in yourself, to have reverence, not to put yourself on a pedestal or think that you are special in anyway—to honor *you*. Collectively, there are over a thousand ways to serve your souls and your spiritual connection. The form of your connection to Self is no concern of ours, just that you have that connection. It does not matter what form it takes.

I get it. Interesting how the questions come up that are about the ego parts of the form.

Yes, and that will continue for a while, until you no longer need it. WE are witnessing the changes in all of you as you claim your power again. As you start to see the Light more often, it brings shivers of joy to our spirits as WE see you singing in your souls again. WE know that most of you have moments of joy in your lives, however, our intention is that you have more moments of joy in your lives. Once you have more frequent moments of happiness and joy, you will experience more of *who you are*, and you will vibrationally lift the level of your Self into a higher frequency until it shifts your planet on a whole. This also shifts your energy collectively into a higher level.

Yes, I get that from Chapter One when you explained the levels.

Yes, that is what WE are talking about. The Light can expand from joy and happiness because all of these feelings are love.

As stated in the Principle title, to have faith is to have confidence and trust in something or someone. Taking it to a more mystical connection to where the naked eye cannot see is to have faith in the unknown. This is your inner soul, your inner Self, your inner being. Have faith in *you*, without conditions, without stories, without external influences. This inner faith builds mountains and timeless effectiveness on the planet. Your ability to have faith can touch not just your generation, but generations for centuries.

Do you remember the saying in the Bible, *Have the faith of a mustard seed?*

Yes, I do. Jesus was telling the apostles that if he had faith, he could instruct the mountain to move and the mountain would move far away.

Yes, that is what WE are expressing to you. Once you have faith in your Self, your thoughts, you can move mountains. You will be able to create miracles of hope and unity among everyone. As Jesus said, once you have faith, nothing will be impossible for you.

Tell them about the faith you have in your clients.

I have such faith in all of my clients because I know if they are coming to see me, they are already ready to change and to release their stories. With the love of God and the faith of their Higher Selves wanting an easier life, all is possible.

WE applaud your faith in your clients, and WE challenge you to start placing that faith in yourself as well. It is always easier to believe in someone else. Now is the time for you to place that faith of a mustard seed into yourself. Everyone is made of the same Source, so remember that you are made of that Source as well.

The line that you love so much in the Course, *We are all made of the same blade of the same grass*, implies that you are all believable and worth the trust and faith you are made of. What gets you all so stuck is your war stories about life. Quit comparing your stories with others. Do not wear your badges of pain…wear your badges of triumphs and victories. WE know you may get caught up in our reference to war stories. Do you not know that even if you did not physically go to battle in a war that some of you are doing battle every day of your lives? It is time to stop the play and get out of the props that are supporting a battle. The reality is that it is not necessary to play in a battle—unless you think it is.

Why not start trusting and having faith in *you*? You alone are the answer. You alone are it. It is your turn to show up. WE are requesting your Light to shine. You are all chosen to bring yourselves and the collective to frequencies you have not experienced as of yet. It is now that WE are holding a symbolic hand out for you. You can do this.

I feel shivers in my body as I am writing this. I have faith that we are all ready to show up.

Wonderful. Tell them the story about your client who was in a coma and the doctors instructed the family to make their final arrangements for their daugther Kelly.

This was over ten years ago. My client called me in despair because her thirty-five-year-old sister was dying and the doctors did not know why. I told my client that I would look at it that night to see if I could do anything. I went into meditation and I brought in Kelly's Higher Self to see why she was dying.

I asked her why she was doing this. Kelly told me she was tired of having money problems and that it was just too hard to raise two small children on her own. Her marriage was falling apart, and the thought that she was going to have to do it all on her own was unbearable.

I had guidance from God to tell her that in two years she would never have money issues again and that she would be doing a great job raising her two small children. I asked her if she were sure that she wanted to leave her two kids who were under five years old. She agreed that she did not want to leave the kids, and if it were going to be easier for her, then she would stay.

I told her she had to completely change the vibration of her body because her kidneys were getting ready to shut down. She told me she would. We hugged and I came out of the meditation. I proceeded to call her sister immediately at the hospital to tell her that her sister would open her eyes in the morning and would be released in a week. I had such faith and knowing that would happen because of the meditation and the time I had with Kelly.

The next day Kelly did open her eyes and she left the hospital in a week. The doctors did not know what happened.

Tammy, remember the all-knowing feeling you had and the faith you had right after that meditation? You also had total faith in your guidance from meditation.

Yes, I did. I did not waiver, and I had no issues whether the family believed me or not. I just knew and trusted what I felt and had faith in what took place in the meditation.

That is it. You were not concerned about what anyone said or did based on the information you gave to her sister over the phone to give to the family. You followed through with what you trusted and had faith in Kelly's recovery before it actually appeared or manifested.

Yes, that is what I did.

Remember, do not have concern about what others think or feel about what you are being guided to do. Your trust in yourself and your beliefs will carry you. It is an energy that is strong and omniscient, and it relieves so many fears from everyone.

Let's continue the story.

Ok.

Tell them the story about Shirley who was at the same hospital only a few rooms down from Kelly when her father died. Tell the story of how this played out later.

I am almost feeling like these experiences in my life just showed up for me to write this book. How weird is that?

Tammy, it is all connected.

I am not sure of the timeline, however, maybe four or five years later, a client called me to tell me her newborn grandson was having major seizures at the UCLA Medical Center. They did not know what to do. My client Shirley did not totally believe in what I did, but she was so scared that they might lose the new baby boy. She also proceeded to tell me that she was only a few doors down from Kelly's room in the ICU many years earlier, and she had heard that I was doing work on Kelly. Shirley felt led to call me. I did not know that Shirley was at the same hospital as Kelly.

I told her that I would see what I could do to find out why the baby was having these major seizures. I went into meditation to see this beautiful baby. He told me he could not handle the energies of this planet and the thought that he had to share a room with another sibling was too much to take on. The mother and father already had four other kids before this baby. I asked the baby what would make him feel safe...and no answer came. I left the meditation baffled, without an answer. That night I had a client and I knew intuitively she had the missing piece. We went into meditation and we still could not figure this out. This was a Wednesday night, and for three days, I was still working on it. Shirley was keeping me updated over the phone. By the beginning of the following week, they were going to bring in a specialist to look at Carter.

I had to go to Whole Foods on that Saturday where I ran into my client Lisa, who I knew had the answer. She told me she brought her dogs into the meditation for Carter and he loved it. I left right away and told Shirley to go get puppy pajamas and stuffed puppies and place them in the crib. I went back into the meditation to tell Carter that he will have his own room with as many stuffed animals as he wants. Carter loved it. As soon as Shirley placed the stuffed animals in the crib, he stopped having seizures.

I knew Carter was going to make it once we got the missing piece, and I thanked my client Lisa for helping. What a blessing that was. Ok, William, why are you asking me to tell these stories?

It is a testament to believing and having faith through God, or a Higher Power, to free the illusions of fear to vibrate correct thinking for others and yourself. Did this not free you as well?

I do not know.

Yes it did, Tammy, because as you freed them, you automatically freed yourself.

I get this in reference to them, but I do not get this in my own life.

Tammy, when you were doing these meditations and you allowed God to work through you, you delivered yourself from the experience of the story that played out for those around you. Do you not understand that feeling safe and asking for help may be the key to "right thinking?" The confirmations you get over and over again are freeing you from your own havoc.

You do get that if you are ever in fear, you can ask for help, right?

Yes I do. I am always asking for help and clarity.

Exiting your life because of a fear of what is to come or what you are creating in your life also means that you forgot to remember who you are, and you completely lacked faith in yourself or God or a Higher Power. Do you believe leaving your planet is the answer to be released from fear?

No, not if it is from fear.

Yes, if you exit your planet because of fear you are creating more ways to learn who you are *not* in order to know who you *are*.

I'm just sighing because it sounds like a lot of hardship and many experiences of learning through pain.

Yes, and this is also a choice you have. Why not choose differently?

I am with you, William.

I know, and it is joyful. So now let's move forward and talk about faith again. Faith is essential in the mix to allow the cake to bake.

What?

Faith is the external not matching what you want to believe in.

I have a question for you, William. What if you wanted to create something in faith and you were not sure if it were coming from love or fear? Can your faith be different from someone else's and is it not all the same?

Having faith and creating from love or fear are two vastly different parts of co-creating. Faith is a choice to trust the unknown without conditions showing up to support your inner beliefs. If your intention is love, you will have a lasting presence of peace and joy around it. If your intention is from fear, then the results will be fear-based. Creating from faith can manifest from fear and love. It is a deep feeling that is felt in every fiber of your spirit. All Light and love is the same, however all darkness is in its own frequency. To a higher power, it is all One and has always been One. Faith, aligned with love of Self, God and a Higher Power, vibrates at a level that is freeing to the soul and heart to the point that automatically brings you joy and gladness.

If you have faith that something external will bring you joy and there is much stress or hardship in your life, then you are in ego and not in your right mind. If you have faith within your being that it will work out and you are not attached to *how* it works out, then you are in alignment with this fourth principal. Nothing will alter the reflection of that energy within, and you will move mountains over and over again.

As WE have explained in a previous chapter, the triumph of the energy of love and joy will be contagious for others to witness to the point that everyone will want to be a part of your experience.

I get this, William, but I also know from my own experience that I have had a mixture of faith in some things and none in other things. Does this make any sense?

What makes sense is whether you could have faith in all experiences and expressions through you from God. What you are saying from your own experiences is that you have had mixed experiences of faith, some of which are from God and some from ego. Many experiences of ego that have happened result in the doom and gloom of life, and you can have faith in that as well. It really is a choice at any moment. What are you committed to believing and what is working for you? Where is your faith coming from? What is your intention? Is your intention from love or ego? All intentions of love are experienced as love and peace. All intentions of ego are experienced as fear and chaos.

Yikes...I get that too. I know most of us do.

So where are you putting your faith? Are you putting your faith into the realms of love or the realms of fear? Do you believe in a heaven on Earth or a hell on Earth? Are you just letting the dice roll to see whatever plays out?

The faith WE are asking you to muster up into your being is the faith that moves all mountains, and everyone moves with you as you do it. As you create the space for God to work through, you are creating the space for God to work through others all around you. You are giving Light and hope and faith to others as you demonstrate it for others to see. You inspire others to move from fear to love as well.

You say we have to learn to release our fears so that we can accept the guidance, right?

You all are on a mission of finding your Light in spite of your egos and the stories you play out. You are all learning what fear is and is not. You are becoming fearless Beings of Light. You are on a journey that is self reflective of Light, and as you become lighter, the darkness leaves. You are learners of the Light and the dark. You are also becoming awake and aware of what fear is and how it feels to live in it, as well as how it feels to live in Light and Love.

You all strive and thirst for love and Light. It is like taking a drink of water that you have been craving. You can only handle small doses of the Light at a time until you allow more of it to go through your spirit.

Remember as you remember You again, you are afraid of the Light as much as you are afraid of the darkness. It requires a systematic flow of the Light for you to undo the fear. You are made of that Light and once you are aware of your Light, you will reach for that Light more often. Once you get to the point that you can contain that Light and sustain it, then you are more than a miracle worker—you are the miracle.

Thank you, William.

Now, having faith is also having the patience of your world's time for things to manifest. Most of you get antsy or impatient waiting for what God has in store for you. The reason that some things do take time to manifest, or for you to see visible signs of your wishes, is that you could not handle it at an earlier time. Things come to you when you can handle receiving them, period. The simple truth is that you were not ready to receive your desires until you know you are desirable to yourself. As your inner psyche is shifted to accept your new beliefs and desires within, the outer will change automatically. It is a match for a match. What's inside of you is always also what is outside of you.

Can you please explain that another way?

You would have destroyed any light-filled events you desired if you did not match the frequency of whatever needed to come in. So, in your own best interest, you held off on receiving your desired result that was of God so that you would not destroy it. So sometimes when it does not work out, it is more than a blessing in disguise, it is a miracle in disguise.

Hmm...

How are all of you feeling about that? Your intention could be that you can ask yourself honestly if you are ready to receive. Are you trusting and having faith that it will be delivered unto you when you are ready for it? Also, the experience that you are desiring must be for everyone's highest good. The pattern of law is that it must benefit everyone. The true victory is that when everyone wins from your experience, then the whole world wins with you.

Waiting for God to deliver you so that you can receive your desires is alignment to God as long as the desires are only of love. Your will is one with God's will. Your ability to have faith without hesitation is also the awareness that you know and believe that without hesitation, God's ability to deliver you into your true alignment of your journey is going to happen in spite of yourself, in spite of the world you live in, in spite of how many lifetimes it has taken to get you to where you are right now, in spite of the stories you held onto for too, too long and are now more than ready to let go of, in spite of thinking someone or something else was your answer until now, in spite of the world's illusions and hardships you have been experiencing. Do you think all of the crises on your planet were accidents? No, they were not, and even in the worst illusions and fear, you have the ability to have faith once again to see the Light of day and the Light of God to have the resurrection and to release all of your crucifixions, once and for all.

WE tell you from our Light experiences, WE are not the only ones who can have these wonderful, joyful, blissful experiences. You can have them too. You shine on us and WE continue to shine on you. Our makeup is the same and the same fiber down to our minute details. WE would not be writing this book if WE did not have the FAITH for you and for all of God's creations. You resemble a Light Being so powerful that if you had faith just in *who you are*, you would vibrate the change needed to change your world. What makes us flicker, flickers the same way through you.

WE see you are now ready to have faith to believe without hesitation that you are that Light Being and are ready to receive guidance. Are you not?

Yes, I do believe we are. I have the faith of the mustard seed.

Ok. Let's move on to Chapter Five.

Remembering One, Once Again

The 5th Principle:
BE YOUR PROCESS IN THE JOURNEY

Know that the outcome is divine order.
Things never really turn out the way you think anyway.

"Be your process in the journey" is being your *own* process in *your* journey. Sometimes it is easy to be caught up in other people's journeys, and you think it should look or be some other way. The ego part of you can lose focus so fast and easily that you may not even be aware of that fact. Can you look at your process honestly and say, "*Do I feel like I am on the right track? Am I honoring myself and others around me? Does my soul feel alive, does my heart tingle? Am I excited to wake up every morning for the new day that is present?*"

If you cannot answer yes to these questions, you are not playing out your greatness. Getting by or just doing what's in front of you will not keep you passionate about life. "Being your process in the journey" is taking inventory of your life presently, not in the past or the future, and asking honest questions.

You are questioning what I am saying because you feel that you are not excited when you wake up every day. Is that true?

Yes, I am not always excited about the day. Nor am I always motivated with joy or excitement. I would think everyone feels the same way. Some days I am excited and others not so much.

Tammy, almost everyone feels the way you do, and that is what needs to be changed.

Ok, so how do we answer yes *to the process and the questions you asked earlier?*

The first question is, *Am I on the right track?* Now this can be a trick question to some, but in truth, it is not. You know when you are on the right track because the Universe is assisting you in your experiences. The right people, places and things show up when you need them. You meet the right person or the right job comes in just in the nick of time to pull you through. The right teacher shows up, the guides and angels are helping you. The reason WE are saying this is a trick question is because even when you are going through hardship, you still could be on track and the right people, places and things show up to assist you.

So we cannot define our process as being on track by the good or the bad or the easy or the hard times?

Yes, do not judge it, because your soul does not know good or bad. Your soul will evolve from the whispers to the thunders of your journey. It is your choice in the play whether you need to learn from a mild experience or a two-by-four. Your experience of growth and transformation can be messy, yet it can be such a beautiful thing. The process changes for everyone as you change. It is ten percent what happens to you and ninety percent how you react to it. The process and your journey will continue to change. Who you were ten years ago may not be the person you are today. This is also why relationships change—you have changed so much that you do not vibrate with that person anymore. WE also acknowledge there are many who stay with the same souls throughout their lifetimes. This means that all of those souls were growing in alliance with each other's vibrations. You will bring in and continue to bring in souls who vibrate with you as you change what you need for your journey.

The next question is: *Am I honoring myself and others around me?* WE know as well as you do that if you do not honor yourself, you cannot honor anyone else. Honor means to have high regard and respect for yourself. It means that you are worth honoring. This sounds simple and it is, however, in practice it is not so simple. Honoring yourself without conditions from your world standards is foreign and a travesty. Honoring and respecting yourself for your makeup as a spirit and soul is essential for happiness and greatness in your life.

Tell them your story about Jacque.

Jacque came to me many years ago totally afraid of spirituality and finding her own voice. Jacque was a joy and such a Light to work with. She started meditating and listening to her inner voice, but she was blocked because she was so afraid her family would not understand her new-found beliefs. So Jacque waited until she felt safe enough to let her family members know what she found joy in. I told Jacque that as she respected and honored herself, the family members would fall into place and respect her for her new way of connecting to herself.

As Jacque found confidence and respect in herself, she opened up slowly to her husband and her kids about what she was learning. It has taken a few years for Jacque to be totally confident, and now her family supports her. A few members of her family are now on their own journeys, asking the same questions that Jacque did many years ago.

As you find your honor and respect for self, you also express that honor and respect outwardly to others. They will either show up with reciprocation of honor back to you or they will fall away, unable to reciprocate.

You do draw in where you are, which means as you honor yourself, those who come into your experience will honor you too. If you do not honor yourself, you will bring in others who do not honor you as well. If you do honor yourself, those souls around you will honor themselves as well. As you give honor to others, you are also giving it to yourself.

Part of the process is asking some basic questions that will keep you motivated and out of fear. Honoring yourself also means not taking things so personally and not punishing yourself or others. Honor means be your own best friend. How would you treat a friend you cared about? You are worth it. How would you treat someone who you loved unconditionally? That is how you can honor yourself. All of these chapters are set up so that they go in sequence to pull you out of your own fears, thus allowing your truest Self to emerge. Honoring yourself also means standing up for yourself with love, speaking your truth to others respectfully and with love.

What about having people around you who do not respect or honor you? Or who do not care what you think or how you feel?

Tammy, to have anyone around you who does not value your soul or your journey speaks volumes. First off, you must distinguish between the unspoken words and unspoken energy. The first step is to acknowledge you are not honoring yourself. Ask us for help. Ask us to help you to honor yourself and others. WE will come in like waves of Light to relish in your salvation and to give order to your honor and your worth. You have a choice to free your patterns back to love. Every situation is an opportunity; if someone is not respecting you, it is because you are not respecting him. You can honor his feelings and energy by releasing him to God. This is your message to ask God to release you as well from your unloving thoughts. Being your process in the journey is owning all your parts in the play, not just selective parts. If you know someone does not honor you, you have a choice to send love to him or her and yourself, or you can continue chasing the pattern over and over again.

Ok, what does "sending love" mean?

It means to send them love energetically, to send thoughts of kindness and love and to really want that other person to do well. It does not mean you have to formally move or give or do anything. Once the pattern changes the release from fear, then you may be guided to be with these people again.

What if you work with someone who is not honoring you and you cannot be out of his physical sight?

What a beautiful lesson it is to learn to honor him before he honors you. This is an unconditional gift that is given to both of you, even if you are the one who gives the gift first. The ego parts are going to say, *"until he acts better, I am not going to change my ways either."* This is a standstill that leaves no one happy or at peace.

Your process is proceeding respectfully with choices set spiritually. This means your choices are respectful and guided by spirit so that you may go through with your days with respect and honor. The process is believing in the journey and that divine order will always be in everyone's best interest. You cannot lose, even if it looks like you are. What is happening as well is that everyone has a set time for things to prosper, and the Universe is lining everything up to match it for you. This information will be outlined more in Chapter Eight.

I am starting to get this to really see everyone well, to see everyone thriving and happy, even my so called enemies.

Yes, Tammy, to see them as any thought you have is to see yourself as the same thought. You do not really have enemies. You have opportunities to be open to love yourself more. The harder the lesson to love others who you do not care to love, the more there is an opportunity for the greatest gift of all. Those people are *you* acting out your worst traits in front of you. They are showing you what is possible in you. They are granting you the gift of forgiveness for yourself.

People you love are also showing you traits in yourself that you love to see beyond the emotional madness you create by your triggers and your ego responses. Do not rush into madness or regret, but hold off for a while to respond only from love. Do not trap both of you into swirls of judgments. Know that there is another way of looking at things.

So I need to be careful what I am thinking about another person?

Yes, be diligent about what your thoughts are. You all know if your thoughts are of love or fear. Remember that saying, *"Treat others the way you would like to be treated."* It is pretty simple in words, and yet very difficult to execute.

The one comment I have, maybe for many, is that you cannot be a doormat, either!

No, you do not have to be a doormat or sacrifice your process in the journey. What it means to honor is to sometimes walk away for a while until you have true clarity, or also to walk away for good. Sometimes to honor yourself and others is to just be quiet and not defend or attack.

Sometimes to honor is to release the story altogether. Hand it over to God. Surrender the outcome and ask for a miracle.

Sounds easy, but when you are in the muck of it all, it is sometimes hard to release it.

Yes, but you can choose how long you want to stay in the muck of it all. Tell them about the dream you had of driving on the freeway.

That was a very insightful dream. I was dreaming I was on the side of the freeway but the dirt road was bumpy—it was not smooth at all.

When did you have that dream?

It was right before the events in 2007.

Then tell them the next road dream you had and when you had it.

Ok, the next road dream I had was right after my conferences in 2009. I saw myself in a car and wanted to cross over a bridge. I knew I wanted to be on the freeway on the other side, but I noticed two large bumps on the bridge. This was exactly the same freeway that I was driving next to in 2007. I also knew I had to go over the bumps to get back on track. I looked to see if there was another way to get to the freeway and there was not.

Tell them the last car dream you had.

The last car dream I had was about two weeks ago. It was about driving. It is kind of bizarre how your dreams tell the truth and how I have not forgotten these dreams.

I saw myself in a car with my friend, and we were on the freeway that I wanted to be on years ago. We were driving forward without bumps or bridges, and the road was straight for as long as I could see.

Even when you saw yourself on the side of the freeway and later trying to cross the bridge in the dream, you were still on track. You could always see where you wanted to be.

That means that everyone knows where he or she should be going. That intuitive feeling is set up to always guide you.

The reason WE are asking you to speak of your dreams, or as WE call this a vision of where you are in your life, is that dreams are also part of your process and your journey. Dreams are maps and messages of where you are and what is happening in your lives. Dreams give intuitive insights to how your soul is moving along. Dreams give messages that take the confusion out of your lives. Dreams help guide you and give insight to your questions. Dreams give direction to what is happening to you as well.

So dreams are also part of the process?

Dreams are part of the messages you can tap into to help you in the process of your journey. Dreams are like treasures and keys to locked chests that open symbolic messages to help you. Why paddle a boat with miniature oars when you can have paddles that are larger and easier to use? Your boat moves easier down the stream. Listening to your dreams and being open to them bring great gifts for you. Once you start to listen to your dreams, you will have unlocked a wondrous imagination of God guiding your journeys. You will know you are not alone in your process anymore.

I do agree with this. I think I take it for granted how wonderful dreams are. I have come to realize that dreams do tell the truth. It is better than a reading.

That is so. Dreams are truth. When you are dreaming, you have released your blocks, your walls, and your stories that thrive on fear. You are pure beings and open to receive direction. Your Higher Selves work through you in dreamtime. Angels work with you as well as all the ascended masters.

Are there other ways we can be true to honor our process in the journey?

Yes, by whole-heartedly believing that divine outcome is one hundred percent for the benefit of everyone. Everyone on the planet, everyone on other planets, galaxies and every living spirit, whatever the form, is entitled to divine outcomes equal to yours.

All of you are divine and your Source within you is much greater than you alone can imagine. So how can your outcome be anything other than divine? You can talk about how this is not working out and this is turning out this way. It really does not matter. What matters is taking ownership of your process in the journey with full gusto. Honor that the outcome is divine and yours to embrace.

Thank you for that message, William. I feel like I just ate a wonderful piece of chocolate.

You're welcome—all of you are welcome.

The next question WE have for you is, *Does your soul feel alive? Does your heart tingle?* If not, then you are not tapping into your joy and you are not living fully. You are probably saying this is not possible, because how many times in your lives have you really felt this way?

Most of you felt this way as a child, more than you realize. That is because you were innocent and felt alive and free. As you have aged and grown up, you have been easily swayed into believing more in the world's hardships and have experienced many painful trials. Just the ability to honor yourself and say, *I have not felt my soul alive or my heart tingle in a long time* will open the possibility for you to bring that joy back into your soul.

Remember that in Chapter One, WE told you about the different levels and that the way to lift your vibrations up into a higher level was to be happy. This is what WE are asking for you to question: What would make your soul happy? What would it take to open your heart up again? Wouldn't it be so nice to say, *I cannot wait to wake up tomorrow to the new day*? These are the kind of questions you should be asking yourselves. Living is just not a beating heart, living is laughing and singing and being fun to be around. Living is also crying and honoring yourselves. Living is expressing your inner child and your wisdom. Living is creating moments of wonder. Living is opening doors you were afraid to open. Living is being aware of others and connecting to those around you. Living is loving what is in front of you right now. Living is freeing yourselves and those around you. Living is loving those for who they are. Living is allowing the changes to happen in front of you without judging them. Living is thriving internally. Living is trusting the play to play out in your lifetime. Living is giving and receiving at the same time. WE could go on and on.

Being your process in the journey requires that you take ownership of your part—that you are a living vessel full of life and choices. It may seem to you that one choice may take you in one direction. However all choices lead you to God in the end. All the choices can turn out in many ways, but the only difference is that some choices are easier than others, and some choices move you quicker along the path to where your soul wants to be. It is like your dream when you were driving on a bumpy road while others were on the freeway next to you, having a smooth ride. It really does not matter what choices you make because in the end will be God. I know you are asking, *Where is the free will*?

Yes, I do wonder that.

So what is your saying, Tammy?

I say, The closer you are to God, there is no free will.

Tammy, you always have free will, but once you are aligned with God, you would not want to live anyone else's will but God's.

Given the conditions of your soul's purpose and your journey, why would you continue to have such hardship on your planet? It is not necessary. You may be asking what is divine order anyway?

Yes, William, what is divine order? Do tell.

Divine order is God's order to everything. God's order is life, breath, energy of Oneness, and divine order is to be open, submissive to God, to put God first in your life. It is God's arrangement of your life. Divine order is perfect, and all who follow it reap rewards beyond your planet. It is inter-dimensional and profoundly beautiful.

Divine order is effortless creativity in your life. It is God expressing through you. Divine order is allowing God to run your ship, not your small self, but your true Self. Divine order is always expressed from the sun rising and shining every day to the moon creeping up in the evening as if on cue. You do not even have to worry about it or even think about it. Who do you think operates all of the things you need to live on your planet? I know you know it is God, but divine order is also expressing itself on your planet. If God can run the bigger things, as you call it, why can't you allow God to express through you the same way? Everything is happening in a state of grace, awe and even wonder.

Asking for divine order in your life is asking, *Are you ready for it?* Most of you do not even know what you are asking for when you do want divine order. It can create so many changes in your life. If you do ask for divine order, it may entail moving or changing your life all together. Divine order is cleaning up or clearing up what really is not working for you in your life.

Are you saying, William, most of us do not know what we are saying? Or what we are asking for?

Yes, when you are requesting help or divine order, you are asking for things to be picked up or for a small clearing. Divine order is not just a little clearing for you but all of the clearing that is necessary for you to be back in with God's order.

Along the way, most of you pick up things, people, and places where the decisions behind your choices were not from love, but from fear. All of those choices will fall away when you are asking for divine order in your life.

All?

Yes, and those decisions that were made from love will stay in your lives.

Can a decision that was based in fear be changed to love?

Tammy, once you allow yourself to think from love, all fear decisions will be healed and will either change and vibrate from love or they will just fall away. As you vibrate from divine order, the fear choices will not appeal to you anymore. You will no longer want, crave or desire that which you wanted before. I will give you an example.

Ok.

Remember your sister and her past when the material world was the most important thing for her? She was at the top of her game, her worldly game. Diana was partner in one of the most widely-known mortgage companies in the world. She had 1500 franchises at one point and anything money could buy. Her wants were of the world and mostly fear-based. As all of that fell apart for her, she lost her business and her husband, and everyone fell away when the money was not there. None of those people were with her when things fell apart? Are those people part of her life now?

No, none of them. So who is showing up now in her play? Remember, those people are not bad for falling away. All of those who have fallen away from her and those who have fallen away from all of you are beautiful souls. Just like you. None of them is bad. Remember, it really is all about where you vibrate from. Her frequency changed and all of those who also changed their frequency are still around her. Her needs changed, so her world changed. It is very simple and required for all of you at some time in your lives.

Now that her focus is on loving herself, what does her world look like? She is married to a wonderful man who loves her for her and not her money. She has two homes that both she and Don love. Her life is simple and her heart is full of love that she did not have before. What she wanted from fear, even disguised, cannot hold a light to what is the real deal from inner love. Once your sister healed and was ready to receive that love, her world fell apart and Diana rebuilt her life on the foundation of love and not fear. All the props that were there before are not there now. New props are now showing up that support her new-found belief in herself. New people are showing up as well.

I so love my sister, William—more than I can say in words.

Yes, Tammy, and she knows it. Your sister believes in you as you believe in her.

One of the key elements in being your process in the journey is to allow yourselves to have an open heart. The ability to stay open even through disappointments is not always easy. WE suggest for you to notice how you are feeling and ask yourself if you are loving yourself and being open to what life can offer you.

As most of you have gone through or are going through life changes, it looks like the carpet was pulled out from under your feet. Keep an open heart about it all, because in time it will prove that the props need to change as you change inside. Within a very short time, you will all see the simplicity of life and what true love is. Living from loving, you first bear fruit of God's vines of life and not the vines of life in your world.

So many of you are going through changes, and WE know it may not be an easy time; however, on the other side of the change is a life full of fruit and tranquility. The only struggle will be if you cannot accept the change. STRUGGLE—Standing, Troubled, Refusing, Undermining, God's Guidance, Losing Ease.

You may go through many lifetime changes—some of which will be joyful and others you may label as painful. All changes are just your soul and heart requesting change long before it happens. The better you are at listening to your soul's and your heart's voice, the easier and quicker you become at moving with the changes. Your soul is choreographing your life purposefully for you to wake up. This forces you to go beyond your limited perceptions of the ego, pushing you through the dark night of the soul. The dark night of the soul is just your ego's way of creating distress and pain. You will no longer need the changes once you have integrated a deep learning and understanding. As alignment of your soul manifests, your expansion grows into the bigger picture. You then have attained enlightenment.

WE know that the process can create such a mixture of experiences for all of you and that is why it is so beautiful to watch all of you as you choose differently. Divine order will create personal fulfillment and peace and finally acceptance.

Another part of the sub-heading for this chapter is, *Things never turn out the way you think anyway.* What WE refer to with this is that most of the time things do not turn out the way you expect. Once you really release the steering wheel to God, your life will change. God's life for you is really different from what you thought you could do. It turns out better and your best thinking cannot put you where God can.

Yes, I know what you are going to say—sometimes it does turn out the way you think.

Do you really know where you are going to be in a year? Do you know how many inner changes you are going to go through throughout your lifetime? Have you ever said there is no way I will live here or there, and then it turns out you end up there? What WE are saying is that because of all of the inner changes you will go through in your lifetimes, you will bring in new locations, spouses, partners, children, friends, communities, churches, etc. You get it. You are wonderful co-creators bringing in all you need to support your beliefs—even down to animals, trees, and the small critters that crawl in your backyards.

But William, I have to go back to the thought that there are some people whose life looks the same as it did twenty or even thirty years ago. Some people have lived in the same houses for many years.

Yes, Tammy, the process includes their changes as well. Do you think that because their outer world is the same that their inner world stays still?

No, but I would think their lives are easier because of not so many changes.

Tammy, many of those you are thinking of who have lived in the same houses for many years or worked the same jobs for many years are also going through their processes of change. What is different is the degree of change they are going through.

What do you mean "degree of change"?

Those people have changes, but they are not so intense. They may not need two-by-fours. They may be listening to their inner voices to make the subtle changes before they become difficult. Remember, it is not what happens to you, but how you handle what happens to you.

I get it.

What WE want to see for you is to not get so focused on results and for you to focus on being present. Yes, you can make some goals, but do not reflect on them constantly. Allow the Universe to assist you in your play. Give the reins over to God. Your soul's alignment to your greatness is breaking through. Do your due diligence in your work. Allow the flexibility of greater things to show up. Your part in the play is so important. New things, people and places show up sometimes when you least expect it. Sometimes that is the gift. Be open to new things.

Many college students start out with one major and may change two or more times before they graduate. How many college graduates are doing jobs that are related to their majors? Be flexible with what life brings in as gifts and don't be judgmental about how the form shows up. There are no accidents, so if one job is showing up and you do not understand it, maybe you do not need to understand it. It may be the people you are supposed to meet there. Always be flexible.

Look at your love life. Be flexible with who shows up. Maybe the package of the person showing up is not what you wanted because he is not six feet tall or she is not a hundred and twenty pounds, or she does not make over a hundred thousand dollars, or he has two kids already. Sometimes those souls are just want you need. Getting to know someone before you decide if he or she could be someone you could spend time with may prove valuable to you. WE see many who brush off suitors because of a list of requirements they did not met. Get to know the content of a person before you brush him or her off. What you are really looking for if you are single is someone to love and honor you, a safe place where you can give and receive love. This is being flexible. Loving someone deeply also means liking him or her. Finding someone who meets your external preferences will not last, finding someone who meets your inner preferences is golden. As you love another, you both can create marvelous creations together.

126

You may have the opportunity to love someone who does not live in your city, state or even country. If you truly love this person, you both can decide to move to be together. Allowing your cities to keep you trapped will not make you happy. If it is divine order, a new job, home and the props will appear to support your change. Have the courage to leap into new experiences. Move to love yourselves more. Move to live. You all know when it is right and when it is not. Have the courage to follow your heart's desire.

This can also run amuck when you are staying too long in a relationship if the only reason you are there is because of the money or the children. If the love is not there anymore, if the form of your relationship has changed and counseling has not worked, then maybe a change is needed. This is when WE see affairs rise up because the need for love is important, but the fear of change keeps you in your marriage. This is an illusion because the hidden truth is that what is needed is not taking place and all parties involved know what is happening. All thoughts are not private. The children know when both parents need to stay together or move on. Kids are very flexible.

William, it is easier said than done.

Not really. Once most people have moved on from a relationship that was not working for a long time, what do you think they say?

I should have done this long before now.

Exactly. You are also holding off love by staying stuck.

Look at all of the people you have met over the years and those who have come and gone. How do you feel about them?

What a blessing to have met some of the kindest and dearest people ever. I think of many often. Many incredible souls have taught me many things. I have such love and gratitude for those who have come into my life over the years.

Every one of those incredible souls came in when it was needed and moved on when it was time to move on. It really is a dance that plays out. Looking back at the top of this chapter, remember when I asked, *Does your soul feel alive, does your heart tingle?*

Yes.

How do you believe you can get yourself to feel alive enough to have your heart tingle?

Do tell, William.

To feel that your soul is alive and to have your heart tingle is to show up. Create a way to feel that you are part of something more than yourself. You may be asking how do you do that? You do that by helping others, by giving of your talents to others, by thoughts, by being present, and by expressing love to others.

As much as WE are saying to honor your process in the journey, you are elevated to a higher level when you give joy and appreciation to others. Allow yourselves to care for others.

You cannot say there are not many people to reach out to. You can reach out to so many in so many ways. You can help your neighbors, your communities. You can reach out through all kinds of services for the children, older people, shelters. What will simulate joy and aliveness in you is to keep hope alive in others. Give what you are craving for. Give what you are desiring in yourself. Give what you would like to see in front of you. Please give without expecting anything in return.

Tammy, do you remember when you gave money to those boys in the park?

Yes, I do and I felt really good about it.

That is what matters. It fed you and replenished your heart with love. The more you give, the more you receive. It is a law of the Universe. To feel alive and to feel inspired, give and share your talents, share your knowledge, share your love. Share what you believe in. To experience the thought to make your heart tingle is to know and believe you have made a difference. You have made an impact on the world or on someone. That is a miracle, and it frees you and whoever else is engaged in the experience.

I get it. This reminds me of the time I worked at the probation department with the kids. I truly believed in them, even when they were locked up. I really enjoyed them and for moments we laughed and enjoyed each other, forgetting the stories or the reasons why they were there. I knew they had the rest of their lives to figure it out. I felt alive working with all of those kids.

That is it. As you believe in others, you believe in yourself. You free both of you, allowing the freedom of truth to swim into your hearts and minds.

What can you do to feel alive? What could you do without allowing the "buts" or the stories to creep in? Think that over. That is an experience that will change your lives for the better.

There will be times in your life where you will require to be alone, then that will pass. You are all made to share your lives with others in all forms and in all ways of life. Engaging with others forms love and experiences you alone cannot create. The reason so many people love their work or their calling is because it is a safe way to love and to engage with others without taking anything away from themselves. It is an easy way to express love and to feed their soul's bank account.

To feel alive by engaging with others is a long-lasting, deep commitment to thriving. Yes, there are temporary props in the play that can make you feel alive and those props are external. You feel aliveness by changing someone's life, by helping someone cross the street, by adopting an animal from an animal shelter, by feeding the hungry. Your actions that display kindness past yourself open others to believe that they can help others too. It also may be talking to someone, helping someone heal, being there for someone when everyone else has walked away. It is the kind of unconditional love words cannot express. You all have had moments like this with someone and afterwards you felt filled up. You knew deep down you did the right thing.

I know time goes by quickly on your planet, and for the most part, you cannot remember the day's events over the years. But what you do remember are the moments that connected you and someone else. That is it.

When you did something that you felt good about and you did not need any feedback from it, that is the aliveness WE are talking about. You have already gotten filled up by helping someone or something. Helping others helps you. Helping others heals you. Helping others releases your stories. Helping others holds you in a space of greatness. You free both of you from illusions and propel you both to higher frequencies.

The next question was, *Are you excited to wake up every day for the new day that is present?*

You all have a new day to start fresh. You can create the day any way you want to. You cannot change the past or even yesterday. The prospect that this is a new day should give you great happiness. It is so exciting to know that this day is a new canvas for you to paint. You can have whatever you want to see happen. What will give you joy and what will feed you? How can you help others? How can you get out of your way to open to new ways of living? What can you do differently to engage your heart and your talents?

For one week, see what you can do every day to show others that you love them. How can you put a smile on their face or inspire them to be different too?

INSPIRE—Igniting, New, Spiritual, Presence, Inwardly, Rising, Energy into others. WE love the slogan, *"Pay it forward."* WE love to see how so many have taken to it and have passed along what someone has done for them. What would really be a joyous occasion would be for you to pay something forward without someone else doing anything for you first.

Inspire others, greet others with joy and smile at strangers. Show a sense of compassion to those having a bad day. Send loving thoughts. Decide that this new day is going to be a great day before you even have your first cup of coffee. Decide that what happened yesterday has no bearing on today. You are not your past any more. You do not have to suffer any more.

It really is a choice to say *no more pain*. You are now showing up no matter what your bank account says, no matter what your love life looks like, no matter what your health looks like, no matter what you are feeling like. You are asking to rise above and to demand a better way. You are asking to see everything differently—all those false beliefs that nail you to your own cross.

Are you with me?

I am, William.

The small stuff that you all get so entangled in is useless and unnecessary. Reach beyond your beliefs. When are you going to get tired of playing so small? When are you going to get tired of the repetition of your wounds that play out such sadness in your world? WE are in agreement with you that you can move mountains. Did you forget how powerful you are? WE have not forgotten. WE will rejoice again and again over your victories of your new-found happiness. WE will continue to see your greatness until you own it.

A new day means a new day. Do not pull up your past any more. Do not believe those who believe you cannot amount to anything. It is just their own beliefs that they do not feel they can change anything. Do them a favor and start anew so they can see what is truly possible in you.

Beyond all of you is the light of greater strength and wisdom that you can drink the waters of God until you are full. Open up your hearts to drink the waters of life that will free you of your thirst. Asking God to replenish your spirits will open a floodgate of miracles. All of you can request God to replenish your spirits in any moment. Drink until you no longer thirst. Why suffer any more?

William, we all want to be replenished now.

All requests are answered in this moment. Do you believe?

Yes, and I am speaking for all of us.

A new day has risen. Now, rejoice in it. Give your life a chance. Live like nothing can hurt you. Love like a child. Dance because you can.

Moving on to the next chapter. Are you ready?

Yes, excited about life and living.

Remembering One, Once Again

The 6ᵗʰ Principle:

LIVE AND SERVE, MOMENT TO MOMENT

Miracles happen in a moment.
If you are passing time, you will miss them.

Watching all of you coming and going in many different directions is like a maze that most of you are going through and getting nowhere. You all look so focused at times, diligently going right and then left and then back and forth. As WE watch you all, WE cannot help but wonder how and when you will stop along the way and just ask for help. Some of you are more determined to try to figure it out by yourselves. WE are here to tell you that you cannot figure it out by yourself, not under the conditions you have on your planet.

As you realize there has to be a better way, it is symbolic of stopping in your tracks and asking for a universal road map to help clear the blocks and fears. You then will be able to see clearly where you need to go. Most of you do not even know where you are headed.

WE are here to tell you that you have finally reached the point where the miracles can happen. Stopping and not moving until you intuitively know what to do will abolish all blocks instantly. This is the chapter that will find you asking questions about how you can serve. What is living about? How can you be open to new opportunities of living?

You are purging your old ways to find new ways. You are ready to receive miracles in your lives. You have come home to your inheritance and are believing once again. To live and serve moment-to-moment requires such awareness. Take all the moments you can throughout the day to be committed, to keep asking how you can live and serve others. How can you serve your Higher Self? That will bridge the gap between the two worlds of the Heavens and Earth. This is your life force of the Light of God working through you. WE are celebrating your process and eagerness to move forward in the chapters, and WE celebrate your return to your Oneness and your consistency into right minds.

You may be asking how can you serve others when you are just figuring out how to take care of yourself? It is not an all-or-nothing motto. The ego part of you will try to convince you that since you can only offer a few moments of time where you can serve, it is not even worth trying. Those precious moments of time where you are serving others or yourselves will be a timeless exchange of healing and recognition of love and the value of giving.

I hear you saying, "I am already living."

Yes, you are living and you may have moments already that you are living, and you are serving. WE say yes, you already do. WE would like to see you become conscious and aware of those moments, because as you become aware of these Godly moments, you will want to create more and more of them. Soon enough you will be creating something greater than you that can reach so many others.

One of the simplest tools to owning your moments in each day is to ask yourself about them. At night, look at the moments throughout the day and see which ones stood out to you. This is the beginning of how miracles take place. As you do this day-to-day, you will discover what really is important.

What is a miracle?

A miracle is a thought or feeling that is of God. It is beyond your worldly beliefs; it is a moment or moments in time that connect you and/or others to an energy that is of God, Light, love, truth, compassion, joy, expansion, and freedom from fear. A miracle is an energy that connects you to your divine Source, and a feeling of

Oneness is present. You will become the moment. You will be the moment. You will be living the moment. Wherever you are, as this is happening, all who are near you will be gifted in the same way because you are never separate from each other.

Tammy, tell them the story about you at the gas station many years ago. You have never forgotten that experience, either.

Yes, I have never forgotten that experience and I believe it must have been over twelve years ago.

I was on my way to work and needed to get gas. I was not too far away from my work place. I was at the pump and holding the gas line and nozzle into the car. All of a sudden, I had a moment where I felt there was some upset energy going on. As soon as I had the thought, I looked up to the inside of the gas station and noticed that a customer was yelling at the cashier lady behind the counter.

I started to pray and send her love. I was intentionally sending her energy of Light and love, and I was also sending the same energy to the man who was yelling at her. In a few seconds, both parties turned to me as if in sequence and stopped in that moment. I felt such love for both of them. The cashier lady behind the counter dropped her mouth open and started to cry. The man quickly finished up and grabbed his bag and came out of the store.

I touched my heart with my hand and patted it for the woman to see. The lady could not stop looking at me. The man kept staring as he walked to his parked car. I felt nothing but love for both of them. This was all done without words or physical contact from either of these two people. The man quickly became soft and full of love. He leaned on the door of his car and did not move.

It was pure love for all three of us. I finished getting my gas, and I turned around to wave to both parties before I left. It was as if that were all that was needed. WE did not need to talk verbally; we had already connected telepathically. I got into my car and drove off and cried because of the intensity of it all. It was joy, and the confirmation I got was that thoughts carry outside of ourselves and that there really is no separation.

Tammy, all miracles connect. No time, space or props you have created can stop them. It is an exchange of love that has no boundaries. It heals everyone and everything in its presence. It requires a pure thought of love to be expressed by one person.

That was your experience. Your intention was only love without conditions and judgment. You filtered away the blocks and fears even if it took only moments to share.

Serving others and yourself is your soul's function. It is a service that does not take much effort or outside requirements to happen. It is a thought and a feeling that is pure. Your pure thoughts of love can change everything in an instant.

How do you feel telling that story?

It touches my heart and gives me chills. I want to remember that experience always. I would love to do that more often.

You can create more of those experiences to the point you will have new experiences to treasure.

William, how do we get to where the energy within ourselves is only love? Sometimes I do send Light and love, and I do not always feel that connection.

The easiest way to do this is to lay down all judgment, all stories, all delusional thoughts that you are trying to fix, heal, do or even create. You just send the feeling and thought because your heart feels the need to do it. That only, is the miracle. You create the situation based only on love. Your mind has changed its perceptions to love and to the moment. Miracles are expressions of love and only love.

All of you have had moments of love and aspire to do great things in your lives. Living inspired lives opens avenues that are not seen yet. It is just like Jesus who walked on water, and his energy alone healed. You all have moments of miracles, and Jesus showed you that you could do that twenty-four hours a day. It is just like the woman who touched the hem of his garment and was healed. That is what WE would like to see happen in your lifetimes.

Why not be like Jesus and allow yourselves to reach for the best frequency you can? Jesus was created in the likeness of God, just as you all were.

It would be wonderful if we could do that.

You can. All of you can if you choose to. Miracles create more miracles and have the ability to change a field of energy far past your physical bodies. That frequency can linger in an area for a while. So even if someone walked into that frequency after the miracle happened, they will feel that energy of love and be changed. They may or may not know what just happened.

Tammy, have you heard of the wall where everyone goes to pray or cry in Jerusalem?

Yes, I have, but I do not know that much about it.

This is a place in Jerusalem where the wall stands today. It is a monument, a Jewish temple, a sacred place for all who want to pray or repent or to release. The energy surrounding this temple has lingered for centuries. The energy of sadness and despair is felt. Many have died here and much blood was spilled here. There is also much energy of hope here, where people leave messages to God for answers.

This is an example of energy that lives on and on. Every day many come to this place to pray. The intention is for a connection to God. All thoughts together hold a frequency around this place because the intentions of those who go to the wall, hold it so sacred and holy that it has become that. It is not the wall or the history that has made it so. It is because the people hold it sacred. WE know the history of the wall and how it still stands.

You are the energy that holds many sites in your world sacred. You are the holy ones and the glue to all matter. Hold appreciation for your places that feed you or give meaning to you. The utmost truth is that you are holy ones, your Light and soul and spirit fuel all meaning to your lives.

What was inside Jesus to do the miracles he did was the flow of the holy spirit. Jesus chose to open his mind and soul to be fed completely by the Light. You have that choice to open your mind and soul, just like Jesus, with the willingness to allow something greater than you to flow through you. It was not the water or the places he walked that created the miracles. It was Jesus who was holy, and that is where you want to focus your attention. The internal(vertical) vehicle of Jesus was pure Light and it automatically shifted the external(horizontal) frequencies. Light always, always lifts and transmutes darkness.

It is grand that you travel to see the pyramids and the stones and go back to the crying walls. It is wonderful that you take pleasure in meaningful places on your planet. First, recognize that those places have meaning because souls like you in past and present centuries created those sites. That is what you want to know about. Who were those people who created such marvelous things? How did they do that? What desires and drive did they have to create such marvelous wonders? Did those souls grow, and how do you feel around these sites? Ask the questions, request an answer. Your species created all things of your world. The wonder is not the things in your world, it is the souls who were driven to create those beautiful things.

Look at your planet and ask how it was created. You created your planet. Your Source at one time was one with God. The ego part of you created your world. You will spend the rest of all of your incarnations trying to return to your original state with God. You were part of God in the creation of your world; however, the other part of you that was ego separated to experience what was not of God.

WE know this may be confusing to some. The miracles are unlimited for all of you to have. That is the miracle. That is because your Light, your souls rejoice in miracles. Your souls hunger for moments of miracles.

As the Course in Miracles says, a change in perception is the miracle. That is necessary for the miracle to take place. But just like Tammy's experience, three people were touched by her thought and her love to expand and share. Her change in perception engaged two other souls that day who showed up exactly at the right time to experience Oneness.

138

Tammy knows she is not special. Everyone can create and can create much in one lifetime.

I do know I am definitely not special at all. I also know everyone is special too.

What is your legacy? How do you feel you matter in this lifetime? What do you want to be remembered for? How are you impacting your family, friends, communities and world?

Tammy, do you know why your friend enjoys going to funerals?

No, I don't, and yes, I do have a friend who really enjoys funerals.

She enjoys them because she witnesses the beauty of the moments of how people are appreciated. She witnesses people sharing stories of the soul who has shifted to another realm. Your friend engages the energy of love that is freely given at the services. It gives her meaning to what is the most important element of why you are incarnated.

What's that?

You matter. Your life matters. You touch people lives. You can matter as much from love or matter as much from fear—your choice. Your incarnation matters. You are loved. That is the miracle—you matter.

I get it. I know my friend Audrey feels connected to all of those people she sees. Now I have to say she does not go seeking funerals. She only goes to the funerals of people she knows. She also does not wish for people to cross over so that she could go to their funerals.

Of course not.

The energy of love and appreciation at funerals can be shown without someone dying. You can show appreciation to everyone, even strangers. That is a miracle, too.

So William, it is really all about loving and showing appreciation to everyone. You cannot give what you do not have in yourself.

Yes, it is a glorious start. That is why you are building your own worth, input, and love first within yourself. Appreciate yourself. Own your own truth first.

How about the energy focused on one person like Princess Diana? Or George Bush?

What?

What energy was focused on Princess Diana?

I can only speak for myself. I loved her without knowing her. As for George Bush, I did a lot of forgiveness of myself for my judgments about him. I also know he is me.

Ok, the honesty helps here. Most of your planet's love for Princess Diana was very evident. When she made her transition to the other side, the love that was expressed from your planet shifted. Many connected to what was real. People were more aware of love for weeks and expressed it freely. Princess Diana was deeply touched by how many people loved her. She did not recognize it when she was in the body. Her effect on your planet is one of love, and Princess Diana is an example of a soul trying to find self love.

As for George Bush, your last president of the United States served his soul's purpose. It may not be what you like or your beliefs, but remember you will learn from joy or pain. George Bush is liked and not liked by people around your planet. George Bush discovered a way to be known and be of service, even if you do not agree with his beliefs.

WE are not asking you to judge others, WE are asking you to be open to your own purpose and how you can be of service. What one soul's mission is, is not yours. Worrying about what others are doing takes that energy away from you, affecting your own purpose. Bring the energy back to you so that you can muster all of that energy, courage, strength, and love for your life purpose. Let your actions demonstrate your energy of love.

I get it. I also know that when we do not understand someone, the easiest thing we do is judge or project.

Yes, you do, and it is not necessary. It uses unnecessary energy—you can direct it from love instead.

Do you think most people feel appreciated?

Hmmm. I do not know.

No, most people do not think they matter, and others think they matter maybe sometimes.

The miracle here is that you can show others that they matter and as you do that, you matter too. You can show them you appreciate them as well. This is an example of service. To serve others is also serving yourself. To serve is to give and to show you care.

WE are hearing your thoughts, Tammy. You are asking, can a miracle happen in a moment of pain?

Can it?

Yes, it can. By expressing your feelings and releasing, you can have a miracle.

WE remind you that you will learn from pain or joy, and miracles can happen in a pain cycle. Your soul thrives on learning and growing, evolving into its brilliance. Do not be concerned about how to set up miracles, relax, ask to come from love and ask for the assistance to release all stories. Can you do that?

I know we are willing to.

The only thing that can change to love is this moment, not yesterday or your tomorrows.

I get that.

Live each day as if it were your last day. Live without regrets. Can you do that? If you have regrets, request a healing, request a new thought about whatever you are holding back from.

Requesting the love of God to live through you will cease your pain and will allow much laughter and peace.

It is so amazing how you see all of the buildings around you from New York to London to China, buildings that have been around for centuries as props so you can remember again who you are. Those buildings and all of the props were set up by you to rediscover your souls' connections to each other. Just do not get so attached to the props you have created. This allows many souls to move in and out of your props much easier. The energy it takes to love is so much easier than the energy you create to separate yourselves from Light. What you are all resisting is the Light force of God within you. You say, how can I handle that much love? The miracle is that you are already that much love without the buildings or props you set up to find it.

WE are talking about passing time conditions on how you can handle love. When I buy that house, when he/she loves me the way he or she should, when I lose the weight, I will be happy and love myself. I will be happy when my mother or father loves me or when I move or get a new car. You can fill in the delusional blanks. That is passing time. A way of becoming present in the moment is to accept your life as it is right now in the moment. Be okay with how things are right now. Own your experience with gratitude, even if it is not where you want to be.

That can be hard to do.

You can make it hard or easy—that is the only choice you have. Accept fully what is and be appreciative of it. How can you make this moment, this day the best? Take in fully how you are expressing yourself. The most important thing is to try not to project your problems on to others. Take responsibility for how you can be happy, no longer blaming yourself or others. There are no victims in any situation. NONE. Your energy is now ready to master the moment-to-moment, day-to-day experience.

William, I am so dedicated to getting this. I no longer want to learn from pain.

Tammy, along with so many others, you all want to learn from joy. The suffering of the souls on your planet is a travesty and a waste of time. What WE mean by that is that the cycles of despair are now appearing in Earth changes, and your planet is showing signs of your despair. Your Light can change that.

I am constantly vacillating between love and fear. And with all of the changes to try to stay out of fear is difficult. It sometimes feels unnatural.

It will feel like that at the beginning, but once you have more moments of love, you will realize the untruths of the fear that bound you all. Your moments will reflect that love. The fear will fall away, and you will relish in joy again.

William, you talk about live and serve in this chapter. Can you tell us more please?

Yes, to live is to love. To serve is to give. To love is to love self, everything around you. To serve is to give of yourself without expecting anything in return. To serve is to deliver with heart-felt love, with compassion, with empathy, and joy. That is why it is so important to find love in self first. Live your days with joy and with reverence for service. It is a gift for you to be incarnated in your bodies to fully express yourselves. Your opportunity to live is a gift from yourself to show who you are.

I never thought of it that way.

Do you believe you incarnated just to express and remember who you are?

No.

That is right. You incarnated also to serve, to live, to love, to express, to heal, to learn, to experience that which you are not.

What?

You also incarnated to express what is not love in order to know what love is.

Hmm. Sigh.

Yes, there are many ways to discover the truth and to discover what is not truth. Once you are tired of the pain cycles, you will return to love.

I do get that. Can you tell us more about passing time? You mention in the sub-heading that if you are just passing time, you will miss miracles.

I wondered when you were going to ask that question.

Why?

When a soul is passing time, it has become trapped in a worldly prison. What WE mean by that is that the soul has given up and is operating from the repetition of life and daily obligations. Does that sound familiar?

What do you mean?

Remember when you were working twelve to fourteen hour days for years? What happened?

It all changed. I felt obligated to work that many hours. I became a workaholic. It freed me from looking at myself. The more I worked, the more obligations came in, to the point where everything changed. I did enjoy my work and I still do, but when one area of your life becomes too much, your soul will create another way in spite of your efforts to keep doing something too much. I kept compounding the same lesson. My soul created a way for me to see what was really important. I could not even look at what was happening until my life slowed down. Once my life slowed down, I realized that my work was not the most important thing to me anymore. My life was important, my family was important to me. I still work, but my work does not run me anymore—I run it. I had to look at myself, once and for all. The last two conferences were not fun for me, and I was barely hanging on just to survive. I was deeply tired and afraid when I produced them.

I have to say I loved the work I did and still do. My work feeds me, but your work cannot be the only outlet that feeds you. Once I realized that, many avenues started to feed me and that is when I knew I was becoming healthier emotionally.

Yes, it did, because your soul required it to live. Your life now is completely different from how it was three years ago, is it not?

Yes, it is. I am much happier. William, there are many who do the same job every day and live the same lives every day. How can you not get trapped, feeling like you are just passing time?

Yes, many of your population are bound by responsibilities to take care of their needs by working or serving. If you get to a point in your lives where the joy has vanished, you feel your life force is gone, you feel numb and not able to feel your emotions anymore, then you are an example of passing time. You become negative and look at your glass as half-empty all of the time. Most of your souls will create a new opportunity to just live on your planet. Some souls will cross over. You cannot just pass time for too long. Your soul will not survive.

I get that. I really do. I see this a lot when a married person will create a situation where the other person moves out to survive. I am not agreeing with it. I see it a lot in my practice. There are many other reasons for change in a marriage as well.

Tammy, there are many ways a soul will re-ignite its fire, its passion, even if it does look like a wrong way. Tell them about John and how he created change in his life because he could not pass time anymore.

I do believe John also was in a lot of pain.

Tammy, just passing time does create a lot of pain as time goes on.

Ok. John had a great job at a telephone company and was very responsible. He was married and had three children. John was living the American life. That is what it looked like from the outside. He had the new home, car, boat, family, friends, but from the inside, John was extremely unhappy and tired of the same thing playing out every day.

I got a call from a desperate woman claiming he never came home from work that night. For the next few days, I was in contact with a family member. To this day, no one has ever found John. This is an extreme case.

Tammy, all cases of passing time will get to an extreme if no changes take place. The way to know if you are just passing time is to look at your life's experience and to ask some fundamental questions: Are you excited to wake up every day? Are you happy to be living? Do you feel like you are living your purpose? Are you numb, apathetic and not happy for a long period of time? WE challenge you to live, to thrive, to see another way, to think another way. You always have a choice to be happy. You are the choice. If what WE are saying does not work for you, then what will? Take the story that if you need to live or make changes, it may hurt others. Creating you, your soul, your senses, brings gifts of change and you are ready for it.

I have to ask this question, William. Many of us have responsibilities to our families, our work place, our lives. How do you just change things? It comes off as being rather selfish.

Tammy, the selfishness is living in a body that has not been happy for a long time. Remember, love is not sacrificing you or anyone else. Taking responsibility is asking God to show you the way so that everyone involved wins, including you, no matter how it plays out. Love is not staying with someone when you are deeply unhappy and nothing has worked. WE have talked about this in past chapters—no job, person, place or thing that takes more than you can give is loving to yourself. You either find a way to make it work or you change it.

Your value is you—period. Your value is not your job, house, car or even your body. You are it. What makes you tick, your soul's journey to finding peace matters. Peace is one word that delivers an inner experience you all want. Are you at peace? Are you deeply happy?

WE also want to reiterate that if you are unhappy for a few months, this does not apply. If you are not happy for a few months, you still can talk to someone. WE are talking about deep unhappiness that you have experienced for a year or longer. Catching your red flags, as you call them, way ahead will be a lot easier to release. Listen to your intuition. It will guide you.

I know you are asking what you can do to prevent getting yourself trapped if you are doing the same job, life, partner, etc. To all of you, there is a simple answer—have fun. Change your life up a bit. Go on vacation. Go see a place you have never been to before. Most of all, find out why you are not happy. Deal with it.

Do not crucify yourselves anymore. Get happy. Own your feelings and ask to feel yourselves again. Release and forgive. Forgiveness is golden.

Tammy, WE love the question you give to your clients: *What would you do if you had all the money in the world?* That question releases all of the fears to allow the play back into a soul's experience of love.

Let's get to a lighter note about miracles.

Ok.

Why do you believe miracles work?

Because it gives validation that you are open to them. It crosses two worlds.

You are on to what our answer is. Miracles give a shot to your soul's journey. Miracles are like giving a shock to your system. Miracles are love injected into your psyche and to others involved around you and not around you. Miracles heal on many levels. Miracles transcend time and space. You will become accustomed to miracles, and as you do, you become the miracle worker.

You become the miracle for those around you and to yourself. Your love and Light will reflect that. You will be opening the door to your greatness. Your Light will change the world. One miracle will lead to another and another. You are more than entitled to miracles. You are the miracle.

William, the Course in Miracles says that purification is necessary first. If miracles are not happening in your life, then it is because you are blocked. It says that we are entitled to miracles.

Yes, as the Course says, purification is necessary first. What that means is that you have a choice to release unwanted thoughts about fear, to extract those blocks that hinder your ability to hear the Holy Spirit, to take ownership in letting go of what is not serving you anymore to finding a way to release. It could be through counseling, journaling, chakra clearing, forgiveness, affirmations, intentions, praying, sacred ceremonies, healing sessions. The form does not matter—whatever works for you. It can take an instant or a longer period of time to clear. You will know when you are purified, because the miracles will start appearing rapidly in your life.

WE love some of the styles you choose to heal from.

Like what?

You can heal through singing, dancing, yoga, tai chi, walking, sitting still, meditating, yard work and knitting. Many of you are healing by sewing, driving, cleaning, hiking, walking labyrinths, being in a sweat lodge and drumming circles. WE see many souls who are yelling and screaming out feelings, or even getting massages. WE could go on and on about the modalities of healing. You know there are many ways to heal, some are everyday chores, cleaning your homes, washing windows, washing your cars and cleaning out your dresser drawers or working out in a gym. Healing is a release of negative energies of fear-based emotions that are released and transformed into nothing. Sometimes you know you have done this and sometimes you do not.

WE must tell you that once you find a vehicle to release and to purge your blocks, it may work for a short while or for a lifetime. Changing your form of releasing is necessary. It is never a one-time deal or a three-month practice. It becomes a life practice. As you live on a planet of fear, your spiritual survival will require you to have a daily practice of some sort to keep you lifted from the plagues of your world.

Tammy, tell them about your chakra experience many, many years ago.

Wow, that was so long ago.

Yes, and that method still serves you and so many others.

Yes, it does. I am kind of embarrassed because I did not even know what a chakra was at that time.

No judgment.

Ok. I was in meditation in early '96 at my home, and I heard a voice that told me to commit to thirty days of clearing out my body and chakras. I was told to buy groceries only as needed. I knew I wanted to be healed, and I trusted this voice and knew it would work.

For thirty days, I came home from work and for two to three hours, I was shown in meditation how the guides and the ascended masters cleaned out my chakras. I watched for hours to see all of the stuff coming out of my chakras to the point I got tired of watching. I could not believe how much I was releasing. Now the ascended masters keep telling me to not value what was leaving my etheric body, but to put value on the replacement of the love that would fuel me. What was leaving was fear and did not need to be judged.

After a two-week period and at the end of the meditation, I completely broke down and cried like I have never cried before. I released so much. About an hour later, I was exhausted and went to bed early. I can say that those thirty days that I committed to clearing were the most connected times of my life to this day. I still use that method of clearing that was given to me by the masters, and I created a CD about it. The blessing to share it has been such a treat.

There are wonderful methods and modalities for you all to use. Listen to what you are inspired to use. WE are suggesting that for you to heal you need to breathe better. Live a life worth living.

William, all of this information sounds so basic. Why is that?

It is because the truth about healing and vibrating from the levels that can change your world requires basic truths that have been around forever. Keeping it basic drowns out any confusion and the ability for peace to hold. Anything too complicated allows the ego part of you to hold on and run with it.

It will take much practice for you to commit to a practice that will alter your minds to God's. It will require discipline and consistency. WE enjoy showing you a way that is easy to understand.

What if you think you have missed your miracles? I know someone will have this question. Also, can you get your life back on track to receive the miracles to co-create? The ego part of our mind will say, I have screwed up so bad already. How can I change it now?

This is a trap that works on many souls. You know you cannot change the past no matter how difficult it was, fault of your or others. What WE would like you to know is that you can be the best parts of your incarnation no matter what day or year it is. All you have to do is say, *I am now getting back into alignment with my soul's purpose. I am no longer willing to play small. I am willing to serve and allow God to heal me so I can be what I need to be for myself and others. I am now willing to show up fully today as an expression of the Light of God.*

Sounds like a winner, William. I love it.

You should—it is who you are.

Why do you think all of those great movies you have watched were darkness fighting Light and Light fighting darkness?

Why?

Because you are doing the same. What it comes down to is that you do not have to fight anything. You just have to surrender to it. Do not give it so much power. What you resist persists. How do you surrender to it? By saying, *so what if I lose my job, so what if I lose my home? So what if you do not like me? So what if I am sick? So what?*

Own it and move into it. What are you learning from it? That is the only reason why situations occur. What are you supposed to learn from this situation, this person, place, or thing? What are you supposed to heal in yourself? What are you supposed to see in yourself? What are you supposed to hear in yourself? What are you supposed to feel in yourself? What are you supposed to THINK about yourself? THINK—Thoughts Having Inner Negotiable Knowledge. All thoughts are subject to change.

Once you start asking, *"What am I supposed to learn?"* your hardships will change and grow as you evolve. Your lessons will slow down, because the repetitive lessons will cease all together.

I know we like hearing that.

The extra work you are repeating over and over again will be diminished. It is much easier to ask the questions when you are not creating hardship.

I agree.

As you ask the questions more and more, you will be in the moment more and more.

That takes an awareness as well.

Yes, it does. If you were not aware, you would not be reading this book.

A huge sigh...I do understand.

Awareness starts with just one thought: There has to be another way. What you are doing is not working and you are finally ready for a change.

For Chapter Six, WE do believe and know that the message has been covered, and you are now ready to move on to Chapter Seven. This next chapter will have you thinking differently. Are you ready?

Yes, I believe we are.

Remembering One, Once Again

The 7th Principle:
THERE ARE NO MISTAKES

You are always connected, so you cannot get lost.

I know that you may or may not agree with this principle. If you just hear us out, you may think differently. There are no mistakes EVER, as long you are a part of God. To better understand this is to visualize a rubber band. If you pull that rubber band out, it may not be the same as its original state or be the way it was made. But if you release it, it will go back to its original shape and the way it was made.

You are somewhat like a rubber band. You are your original state, which is one with God. However, as you expand your thoughts to fear you will pull away from your original Source and stay there until you are too uncomfortable.

To say you make mistakes is misleading because you can never leave your Source. That is what WE mean when WE say that you cannot get lost. Your essence is pure love, even if you do not believe it. You may contract or expand or get weak through your own choice. You can never leave or destroy what you are made of. You can also leave your body and go on and still you cannot destroy your original state.

WE can assure you confidently that you cannot make any mistakes.

What WE can tell you is that you can make your life harder and very difficult, or you can have a peaceful life. The reason it does get harder is because you are acting out of accord to who you are, which is perfect love. If you allow what is not you to appear—your ego—then you will create disharmony. Again, you will do that until it no longer serves you.

153

WE know most of you are thinking, *Why would I intentionally choose pain and to push away from love and peace?* Because of the worldly thoughts and stories you buy into. Because of deep wounds and patterns you have recycled over and over again. WE know most of you do not intentionally hurt people, yet there are those who do. It is a strong suggestion that your model of operating is not working on your planet.

The word *mistake* means to be misguided or to be wrong. From the perspective of truth, that means that you may have taken a road that may make it harder to get the lesson. You are really learning what your souls want to learn. Each experience will show up as a whisper or it may come in like thunder. It really is not important how you get the lesson. The most important thing is that you got the lesson—the light bulb went off. Lessons can take from moments to years or lifetimes. Some of the best lessons you learned where those you believed were your most difficult times. But you can learn lessons from joy as well.

It says in the Course in Miracles that a mistake means that you "missed the mark." Taken in that interpretation. How would you look at that? What are you going to do now? The ego is so clever at getting you so hung up on how you missed the mark that it paralyzes you into not moving out of it. So what if you missed the mark? What would a marksman do if he aimed his arrow at the bulls eye and did not hit it? What would he do? Yes, he would try again, maybe standing differently or moving his hand or elbow differently. That is the same for you. You can try again and try another way.

Another reason the marksman reacts so easily to pick up another arrow is because he can see another arrow is there. Symbolically, so can you. Your spiritual arrows are lined up for miles, just waiting for you to pick another and another when needed. The supply of universal miracles is endless and has always been there for you and everyone on your planet.

For instance, that may mean that maybe your job is not working for you, so what do you do? You try another job or try to open another door to what it is that you are supposed to do. Do you think a marksman would get hung up over what color his bows are or the tips of the arrows once he knows they are fine?

Once you know the job is not it, stop and do not get so fixated on why the job is not working. That is not going to do anything but put your energy into misery, where the ego wants you to be. If you had a friend come to you when she was so sad and upset because she knew her job was not working for her anymore, what would you do?

If you are aware and full of love, you would suggest that she look for another job and move on, would you not? But what if your rubber band were pulled out just like hers? You would probably get all caught up in the story and go on and on about what they did to her. You would project and blame. Where is that going to get you? If another person comes along whose rubber band is its original state, that can help pull you both out of fear and back to love. One person has to come from love in order for there to be order.

This is basic, and that is what needs to happen. You can ask yourself if you are in your original state. Are you pulled out of shape from your stories, or not? Now before WE move forward, you may not want to hear this, but there are souls among you who love to be in pain, who thrive on the drama, who feed off of your story so that it justifies where they are in their lives. If you get into this frenzy, please remove yourself from the crowd and go get quiet. What is going to really make you happy?

Get beyond the story and ask what you are supposed to learn from this. And please take one problem at a time. Problems are issues you have created for yourself to experience. Yes, you create everything. Can you understand that you created all of your problems from the time you were born to the time of your death in every lifetime? The wonderful truth is that you can solve all problems easily. It really is very simple.

WE will give you an example.

Tammy, your son's accident was created by him. As WE get into this, WE will also explain that even though it was James's choice to have that accident, you also agreed to be a part of his recovery. How do you feel about that?

I do get that, but why would we agree to do that?

James wanted an opportunity to wake up in a way he could not do before. Remember WE said that you will have whispers to thunders.

Yes.

James did not listen to the whispers, so his soul created that accident along with the three other passengers in that car in August of 2009.

I am just breathing through this. Crying.

Tammy, James learned deeply about his life and what matters, and maybe he has not implemented all that he learned from that accident as of yet, but he will. You will see his life change soon. James does not remember any of the conversations WE had with him when he died and came back, but his soul remembers.

Should this be in the book?

Why not?

I know James has many questions regarding this accident, problem, lesson, whatever you want to call it.

Yes and WE know his soul and spirit. James will have answers in this lifetime to some of the questions, and there will be questions he may not have until his crossing. You may understand this or not, but many questions may not be answered to your liking. The best choice is to make changes when necessary and to be accepting to what you may not know.

Huh?

Tammy, many things happen to all of you in your lifetimes that you may need to learn. Those lessons may come from different lifetimes including the future lives and past lives. It also affects all souls on all planets. Your ability to try to get answers may even create more problems. Be diligent to learn what you can and allow God to flow through you to heal what you may not even totally understand. The goal, if there is a goal, is to be at peace and come from your right mind to heal yourself and others you come in contact with as well as those you do not.

You are saying, William, that we may not have all the answers to some of our questions? Why not? Why do we have to have the veil over us before we incarnate? Why does it have to be so damn hard sometimes?

Because you all have set it up that way. You also wanted to go to planet Earth. There are endless numbers of galaxies to go to. You all chose Earth. There are many planets that are much easier to live on.

Why would we choose Earth if we could have had an easier life?

If you don't see the duality of other beliefs, you cannot appreciate other places, souls and other journeys. Your soul is experiencing the duality within your planet. You all have lived on other planets, galaxies and even were guides at some points of your journeys.

Why would we want to experience that duality just to appreciate other places?

Tammy, you are also experiencing the false beliefs of the ego in order to be your original state as well. You were all eager to incarnate to be what you are not, in order to value what you are— life, God, joy, peace, Oneness. You agreed on a collective level as well. Remember, as you light your planet, it lights the other planets, stars, galaxies and the universes. Your planet is requesting a healing by all of you, because you are your planet.

You have asked for and jumped at the opportunity to live and be on your planet. Your soul wanted a chance to live where there is duality and dark and Light, knowing always that the Light will prevail once and for all. As you are living in your bodies, you have forgotten that.

On your planet, the veil is being lifted. Every year it is getting thinner and thinner. WE will talk more on that later in Chapter Ten.

Ok, now back to this chapter. One of the problems WE see you create is that if a situation does not work out exactly as you would like it to, then you will sink into a lower frequency and create other problems. One of the ways to clear out illusions is to remember that any time you are looking outside of yourself to be happy, you will not be at peace. That alone will create much distress. Your true happiness is within always—no ifs, ands, or buts.

William, you are saying that if I am constantly looking outside of myself for happiness, it will create more problems, right?

Yes, until you get that the truth is not outside but inside of you. Let's give another example of how problems create themselves.

Ok.

Have you ever had a bad day it creat and compound more problems throughout the day?

Yes, I think we all have had those kinds of days. I was at the point where I just wanted to go back to bed, hoping for a new day to start.

Remember when you were a child and your family went to pick up a load of cantaloupes out at the farm? Once you were all loaded, the truck would not start, and you were all stranded from 8 in the morning until 11 that night.

I remember that once we got the truck fixed later in the day, we had to drive home slowly. We were about three blocks from the house, and when we turned the corner down from my house, the axle broke off and the cantaloupes went all over the street. I was about twelve years old and could not wait until we all got home. We were exhausted and tired from that day. It was one thing after another. We laugh about that now, but it was not very funny going through it.

Tammy, that is how you can operate and sometimes you do create more problems over and over again, one right after the other.

And there are times you do get your innocence and enjoy your days. In this example, your mother knew not to use this truck in the first place, because it had been sitting for a long time without running or being serviced. Your mother did not listen to her intuition.

Yes, sometimes we do not listen to that intuitive voice. The start of all illusions and problems is that you knew ahead of time and did it anyway.

That is the inner voice telling you something so you knew ahead of time. Ask your mom and she will tell you she knew but she wanted those cantaloupes and would not settle.

There are no mistakes—only problems that can create more problems. The joy is that you can stop all problems by asking for help and taking the time to listen to what it is you are supposed to do.

Tammy, do you remember that situation where you were in a contract to buy that five-unit apartment building and you felt like someone was not telling you everything? You did not have the information, you just knew it. You felt it. Why do you think you were open to the answer?

Because I was not attached to having those apartments at the cost of sacrifice.

What did you do?

I had a hit intuitively to call the bank who owned the apartments to ask what was going on because the price of the place kept going up. I did ask God for help and told God if it was for my highest good to have the apartments, then let it work out. If not, let it fall apart. I was concerned because I did put a large down payment on the units and I did not want to lose my money.

When this wonderful lady answered the phone, I told her what was happening and I did not feel there was much honesty going on. The lady looked over the loan papers and discovered the agent involved on their end had included all the delinquent payments for eleven months including the late fees. Once the lady on the phone saw this, she got permission to refund all of my money and the loan

REMEMBERING ONE, ONCE AGAIN

was null and void. I got back all of my money on the loan and moved forward. This was done over a ten- or fifteen-minute conversation. The problem was solved very quickly. I had my money back in about five days.

I forgot about that experience.

Once you ask for help, order in your life is on the way. You have opened the bridge to any difficulties involved with the problem when you ask for help. Your request for a miracle restores order instantly.

I also found out the apartments were infested with termites.

Tammy, this is a story where you created a miracle that changed everything back to peace again just by asking for help. Do you think that lady would have been on the other end of the phone if you had not requested help?

No.

She would not have been in that minute of that day.

Wild how that happens, William.

When you ask for help, WE listen and respond and deliver all problems to the Light. The truth is underneath all of your fears and darkness. Light is waiting for you. Now sometimes it looks like it may take a while for order to appear and sometimes it appears right away. More of that in the next chapter.

Can you put your thought around the idea that there are no mistakes? You may have problems, hardship, despair or even pain in your life cycle. Your only choice is love in any situation—only love. You may not understand it, either. Remember, you are part of a collective force and group of souls also in agreement to show up in the play to play out situations you are not aware of. You also agreed to show up for others in ways that you agreed to experience in order for you to wake up or for them to wake up. The experience may look like pain or joy, that is a choice as well. Would you like to relate or understand a story about how some of you have woken up?

Yes we would.

First off, everyone you've met and are going to meet in your life times have been orchestrated prior to being incarnated. You have agreed to exchange an experience together. The connections you make can come from a cordial hello to a intense connection that could be from prior lifetimes. Tammy tell them about your client Laura who met a man whom she was totally taken with.

I met Laura over fifteen years ago and she was so much fun to be with. I got a call from her not long after. She was so devastated and in such despair. I asked her what happened to her. Laura proceeded to tell me she was at a local restaurant and met a man named John. As soon as they locked eyes, she said she was shaken to her core with emotions of needing to know him. Laura said that John was too afraid of their very intense connection after being together for only a couple of weeks. John did not want to talk to her or even see her again. Laura was mortified and lost. I told her it was a past life experience and that she was now blown completely open from this connection with John. Everyone who knew Laura could not understood her pain or suffering because she did not know John for very long. It took a year for Laura to breath easy again.

Why William would Laura arrange for this experience?

The reason Laura had this experience is because her soul, along with John, agreed to know who they really are past worldly beliefs. Even if they have become too afraid to embrace the experience, they agreed for it to show up in their play. This is a beautiful opportunity to love, heal, and to celebrate each other. It is also an experience to discover your self in ways you have not, to awaken to your heart's, awaken to your soul's essence of life. It is also a wonderful experience to heal a part of you that requires love again. Did you not have the exact experience yourself, years prior to Laura?

Yes I did and I do not wish that on anyone. I met someone and was completely shaken to my core as well. It took me years to recover from that experience. I was blown open and in such pain. That was the beginning of my awakening. I wanted to understand more about what this was and why it happened to me. My friends did not understand why I was taking this so hard. I kept asking

God to show me the truth. Finally one day, I was at the oil refinery I used to work at. I had a vision of a life over a hundred years ago when I was a man with a wife and child. I had just come back from the war and was thrilled to be back with my family again. In the vision, it showed that I had a black woman who worked for me and she was a part of our family. I discovered that my neighbor had raped her. I was very upset and decided to ride my horse to confront this man for what he did. We had words and I told him he could never come on my land again. When I got on my horse to leave down the dirt road, he shot me in the back and I died not too far from my house. My wife and child had to bury me. In the vision, I saw my wife later in years who was still grieving, and had not recovered very well from my passing. So when I saw the soul again in this life time, it was as if I picked up exactly where I was before I was killed. I totally understood then why it was difficult for me to get over that connection in this life time. That vision cleared everything up for me. I no longer had confusion about the experience. I begun to heal very quickly.

You will bring many opportunities to wake up in your life time. When you are open and questioning more than the worldly beliefs to why you are here, then you know you are waking up. You have discovered the treasures of your soul, bringing life to what matters most—you.

Can you give an example of someone who is awaken through joy?

Yes, WE can do that as well. Do you realize when you are with your clients, you are learning from joy? When you are working with your clients you have put your smallness aside to show up fully for their sessions.

Yes I do. It is such a sacred space where there is such intimacy. You can feel the presence of God everywhere.

That is it. You are one with the joy of God. What you experienced was windows of time together that took you into your selfs. You laughed and you cried with each other. You dove deep into parts within and discovered the true Self, when you are with your clients to share the God presence within. When you create a safe place where love is present, you join an inner awareness that is joy. As Oprah says, joy rising.

William I have had this with all of my clients and friends. I enjoy the sharing and the intimacy of God working through us.

The doors of your inner worlds are open. You have chosen not to allow the ego in. These are the golden moments, the reality of life, the force of light that takes you to heaven.

I am blessed.

Now let's talk about redemption as part of the mistakes.

Let's talk about redemption.

Where do you think redemption lies? First off, everyone is redeemable, including you. No matter what happened in your life in the past or present, you can be forgiven and so can everyone involved in the play. There are no victims.

WE are not saying you can do anything and be forgiven and just get away with it. When fear is acted out, there are consequences. There is retribution and an energy present at all times. You may call this karma. WE like to call it the Law of the Universe. What you think, do, believe, or feel vibrates and is constantly reflecting your will and God's will back to you. Your choices will give back to you what you are choosing.

Another way to look at this is to know that every action you take creates a reaction in thousands of ways. The only way you can change this is at the level of the thoughts you agree to. You know by now, your thoughts come from fear or love. Once you change your thoughts to align with God's, your actions will display that. The mind is where the change is necessary. Your thoughts were in place long before you have actively followed through with an action.

It is a Universal Law you cannot change. All of your ascended lives and past and future lives play into this lifetime as well. Say you were very prejudiced against a black person and had much uneasiness towards a black person in a previous life. What do you think you will be incarnated to be? Yes, a black person in this lifetime. You will love what you did not understand in the previous life. What if you killed a person in this lifetime—what then? What happens is that in your next lifetime, you will redeem yourself to that person. You will rectify on a soul level to the act you committed in that prior life.

How would you do that?

You may end up saving his life in his next lifetime. You may be his servant or work under him. You may be his child, and along with him, much forgiveness will surface. You have all lived many lifetimes of redemption. It is time to start forgiving the lessons and issues of this lifetime.

The way to clear up your karma, your actions or thoughts that are not in alignment with God's, is redemption. Redemption comes from God and your decision to ask for it. It may or may not require you to go to those you have hurt. You will be guided by your intuition once you ask for redemption to see them in person or in spirit. Forgiveness is redemption, no exceptions.

All situations can be healed and will be. In the end, everyone will be One with God. There is no problem God cannot solve, but there are many problems you cannot solve even if you wanted to.

You talk about sinning, Do you believe you can even sin?

No, I do not.

No, you cannot sin. You may have made an error, but God sees your innocence. The more you feel you have sinned or missed the mark, the more you will judge it and punish yourself. Forgiveness is vital for your survival. Have mercy on your soul and your life path. Discover the beautiful souls you are. Deliver yourselves from punishment. It is past the cross. It is killing your planet. Sounds harsh, however, it is true.

You cannot be great as long as you punish yourself and others around you. You cannot make any mistakes, just misguided, delusional thoughts that bind you. Let go of the illusions. If you want different results, have different thoughts. Ask for help. WE are going to repeat this over and over again. Keep asking for help. That is what WE are waiting for. A miracle is where you know you need help. That is all it takes.

Some of you are thinking, *Well, so and so has it figured out. He is so far ahead of me.* That is an error in thinking. This may come as a surprise, but your life is not a horse race. You truly can be redeemed in an instant. You can be as awakened as the Dali Lama or even Mother Theresa. Do you think they had hardships? Yes, and the Dali Lama still does. What he does differently is that he forgives more quickly than most of you. Think how hard it would be to be exiled from your own country and to have your beliefs mocked on a constant basis. What lessons is the Dali Lama having? Yes, he has lessons just like the rest of you. There are no free rides for the soul to grow.

What lessons you are learning may not be that big of a deal for someone else and vice versa. You must take into account your family, culture, and environments as well as your up-bringing to start asking what you are learning from your family, friends, environment. Once you ask those kinds of questions, your recovery process is beginning. Your awareness is expanding and opening you up to who you are beyond your bodies.

Remember, you are like that rubber band that may pull away from its original source, but you will always come back. What if the rubber band snaps? This is also symbolic of your transcending into another realm.

WE want to explain how there is a Law of the Universe that is of God and there also is a Law of Chaos.

What WE would like to say about the Law of God is that it is of truth and Light and Oneness. The Law of Chaos is completely the opposite. It is strife and struggle and separation. It is all about your winning at any expense. It is about the illusion that you are a sinner and must be punished and attacked. You substitute love for vengeance and attack. These beliefs will alter your outcomes away from your original state of Oneness, but the Light is never put out. Your Light may be dim, but it is still there. How far down the hole of pain do you want to go? Your choice.

The Law of God and the Universe is that of peace and alignment with who you are. Your Light is bright and your hope is restored and your passion and joy are ignited to give to others. Your love will be felt by everyone, and your service will bridge miracle after miracle. There will be fewer hardships.

WE would like to share another story about being stuck in a learning lesson. Are you ready for it?

Sure.

Do you remember the movie about Harry Potter?

Yes, I just saw the movie and loved it.

You can create so many problems and fears. What the movie and story really relay was that until you face the darkness, the Light will be challenged over and over again.

In the movie, Harry Potter had to face the darkness, and all was healed at the end. In retrospect, you are not much different from Harry Potter, but the darkness lies more within as the Light is flickering to the surface. Can you look at your darkness and know it means nothing? Look at the noise and the false stories you have held so tightly. As much as this chapter is about knowing you cannot make any mistakes, it also is about accepting yourselves as you are. Forgive yourselves because as you continue your journeys, you will have problems showing up from time to time. You will be better equipped to forgive it more quickly and then move forward.

This reminds me of the Matrix movies. I loved those movies too. At the end Keano Reeves allowed the darkness in him, surrendered to it, and then Keano was the light.

Yes, and that is what you can do. Say *so what if I have a few things to work through? In spite of those flaws, I am going to love myself and still show up from Light.* The power of your God Self is much more powerful than anything else.

You have a wonderful journey and new tools and beliefs to lift your spirit up. Knowledge is power and experience is wisdom. The wisdom is vast and equally important. Take your journey with hope and a passion to learn, a curiosity of the innocence in your soul and allow the vastness of your spirit to rise.

You are all in a movement of finding your way into the Light, finding that your Light is within and connected to everything. If you could see how much WE love you, you would jump for joy. In and through you, WE care and deeply believe in your journeys and your survival. Can you believe even for a second how grand you are, how sweet your Source is, how WE savor your victories, how WE see your pain and see your Light? Can you for an instant allow yourselves to be love and to be kind to yourselves? Can you for an instant own your strengths and release your worries? Sit with us in meditation. Come to a place of grandeur in your souls to dare and be brave. WE strive to hold your glory and to boast about your abilities when you have forgotten. WE listen to your stories and sort through the false ones for those golden treasures of truth and Light. If you only knew the armies of God, who stand patiently to guard and protect you from your false thinking.

Can you for one instant allow the troubles of your world to cease? Can you see your world living in harmony? WE know that the harmony has to be within you first. Can you for an instant see every child fed and sheltered, free of pain and all their needs met? Can you see for an instant the glory of your world full of lush green plants and clean air and everyone working together to make sure everyone is taken care of? Can you see for an instant your governments working together for the welfare of your planet, making sure they are walking away with appreciation for every species on Earth? WE see such disdainfully abusive power struggles between all the separate parties. There are more broken parties in your government than WE care to count.

Can they walk away with hope or are they walking away with shame? What messages are you sending out to your planet? When you agree with others that things are screwed up, you have lost your mind. Can you for an instant see all parties working together for the betterment for all. Can you just for an instant realize that there needs to be another way of living and thinking? Can you for an instant ask us for help?

Recover your essence, relinquish your fears for once and for all. See the beauty again in yourselves. See your child-like parts so you can live with laughter again. WE are holding the energy for you to know WE see in all instances your strength, courage, your resilience and your playfulness. Let's play again. Let's jump for joy again. Let's get excited about life again. It is your turn to show up. You can do it. Live past the mistakes, because there never were mistakes. Only you. Only your Light. Can you for an instant remember that? What is it going to take for you to stand up and say, *I cannot do it this way anymore? I, in this instant, am requesting another way.* Once you do this, the so-called mistakes leave like dust in the night. They were never there to begin with.

Now WE are moving onto Chapter Eight. As you can tell, WE are excited with you as you read on. You are discovering your true nature and WE are one with your Light. WE see your changes and are singing in praise. You will witness your awakening as a homecoming. As WE move on to the next chapter, you can see how each chapter supports the next.

Trust in the truth of God and as this book is written and know that the support of the Heavens is with you always. WE support you in spirit and soul. WE bow to you brave souls as you listen to your souls' requests.

Now on to Chapter Eight.

Are you ready?

Yes, and I do believe WE are excited.

Thank you, William.

The 8th Principle:
IN DUE TIME

Things will rise & prosper as you rise and prosper within.

This chapter is the crucial turning point as far as having your desires fulfilled—to seeing your wishes granted. The true aspect is that your focus should be on your process and how you are rising.

The ego part of you will have you focused outside of yourself to see what is tangibly manifesting. The missing part is that the change in perception and the vision should be inward. Where are you inwardly on your journey? The inner is conclusively attached to the outer world. So if it is not working outside of you and your life experience, it is because the inner is not where it needs to be to match your outer world. It really is all about the match in frequency. The accountability is within. Are you where you want to be? What can you do to change your thoughts and frequency so that your outer starts to display what you want to see outside of you?

What is it that you really want? What is going to make you happy? Do you even know what would make you happy? Those should be the questions. Do you feel connected to your Self, your Source? Have you let go of any false beliefs that do not deserve greatness? Have you let go of the past? What are your personal stories that work for you and do not work for you?

One of Tammy's issues about manifesting is that she wanted it too quickly. Whatever she wanted, she was not willing to wait for the right time for things to prosper. The ground underneath her was not as stable as she thought it was. How many of you have been like that?

Tammy has learned the hard way that you cannot force or push things to happen the way you want them to be. The outcome will not be what you want it to be.

Do you have to use me as an example?

Why not? Your experience is everyone's experience.

Ok.

Forcing the results when the Universe has not lined up to match you can be very painful indeed. Patience is a virtue. What patience means is delay. But whose delay is it? The phrase *"everything happens in God's timing"* means that when you are open to the most brilliant experiences from God, the heavens line everything up to match the outcome that will benefit everyone involved. Do you have the patience to wait for that?

WE ask you to be actively opening the symbolic doors to what is for your highest good. But not at the cost of kicking the doors open, or giving up too soon. In due time means letting go of the control of when and how things come in.

Tammy, tell them the story of your one client who needed a job and you both knew it would be down to the wire.

Yes, the only information we both knew is that it would be down to the wire. For over a year, my client worked diligently along with God's help to bring in the exact job she wanted. There were times she wanted to give up; however, she could not give up her ability to take care of herself money-wise. Thank God for that.

A few weeks before running completely out of money, the job she was requesting from God showed up in every way she wanted. The pay matched, the location matched, the terms of the beliefs she wanted to see in the other people was also a match, even how long it took her to drive to that job.

What are you lined up with? Where are you vibrating from? The mirror will never lie. Is your life reflecting what you want to experience? Remember, it is no one's fault your life is the way it is.

If you like where you are, then continue to co-create more of the same. It takes consistency to co-create your desires. And remember, your desires are constantly changing as you change.

WE will give examples of someone who is patiently waiting and believing that God is delivering what the desires are and WE will give examples of when others have derailed their greatness from coming in because they feel they were not ready or did not deserve it.

Ok, sounds great.

First, WE are going to start with someone who sabotaged what was rightfully his before it manifested. Do you remember your client George who wanted to meet a girl and to have a long lasting relationship? Unfortunately, he had a lot of fear of receiving the girl long enough for it to manifest.

Yes I do.

You worked with him for six months.

Yes I did.

Well, George would have had the woman come in within a month after he gave up. George quit doing the meditations, the work to manifest his desires.

Yes, and George was going out to meet new people and I know he quit that altogether too.

All George would have had to do was continue the path he was on, but he got impatient and afraid because his desired results were not showing up yet. The girl did appear about a month later, and he was not around to meet her.

Can George change this now?

Yes, he can. He can change it at any time if he chooses to. George would have to restart the practice of how he learned to manifest and to be able to receive. Changing your thoughts and believing you can have what you desire is the key. George can bring someone else in who was the same match as she was. Giving up just before it comes to fruition is meaningless.

Sometimes the great things that can come in can be too much to receive. That stems from not having enough self-worth, not believing you can receive wonderful things in your life. Part of not allowing yourself to receive is not forgiving yourself or others. The other part is allowing fear to dominate you.

Another example of someone sabotaging greatness is a client you had a few years ago who owned her own medical practice. Jody was just changing her thoughts and frequency to acquire what she needed to run a successful business. She was on the brink of losing her practice, and with your help, her business was just starting to turn around. But because it was not coming in as fast as she wanted it to, she gave up and quit doing her homework. All the necessary tools that you gave her to do on a daily practice were put on hold. What is true is that the inner work is the miracle. Your inner world is always expressing itself outwardly.

This is such a crucial junction in all of your lives that it can feed your abilities to co-create or it can cripple your beliefs. In due time means everything has to precisely line up the same energy from within you to the heavens, to the unseen energies of the Law of Nature, to the people who are dancing around you to play out what you are asking for. If you could witness the details as they come together for you every day, you would be in awe, grateful and inspired to show up better in your lives.

Having the choices you have to select from is vital. Anyone who is wishy-washy will create wishy-washy outcomes. What do you want? What do you desire? WE will say this again. Do you really know what is going to make you happy? If you are not completely honest with yourself, get honest. Put aside the fears around it and just imagine that no one or thing could hurt you. You really could create anything. What would that look like?

Your life is your life. Your breath is your breath. What you do with your thoughts and desires is all you. At some point, you will understand that more fully. Sometimes it takes work and a deep commitment to attain the results. Are you willing to do the work, and are you truly ready to make commitments? Great things do require a focus and a commitment. Are you more committed to not doing anything than to just see what happens? Are you hopelessly hoping for a prince charming to come along and give you what you want? Any delusional thoughts that someone else can meet your needs and make you happy will disappoint you in the end. It starts with you and nobody else. What can you create? Waiting will not bring you the results you are looking for. How long are you willing to wait? You are the one you are waiting for. When are you willing to show up? Most of you keep bumping into things along the way. One question to ask, *"Is this for my highest good?"* and if not, let it go away. Moving and putting one foot in front of the other is vital on your journey.

WE see so many of you finally getting to results that serve your highest good. Taking responsibility to change and the courage to create a new way is essential. In due time is now living in divine outcome. Due time means even when things look messy, sometimes they are working out in your favor. Living a spiritual life that gives growth to the soul is accepting the difficult times and the joyful times.

Tammy, "in due time" is the rise within you. To rise within you means that are you matching emotionally and with thoughts to what it is you and your Higher Self want to bring in. Do you believe you deserve it? Do you believe it is your time and does your frequency match to receive what it is you are creating?

William, reading all of this sounds like you are repeating over and over the same talk, and it also sounds preachy like we are not listening to what you are saying. I just want to be honest about it.

Tammy, WE want you to share the messages, and maybe it is repetitive, and yes, it may sound preachy; however, if that is what it is going to take, then so be it. WE are not here to judge you. You do enough of that on your own. What WE are here to do is bring the message over and over again until WE can break through your egos and stop the rides that continue to go into circles of hell.

WE pray you see the meaning in all of the words written. Tammy, all of you are on your own journeys. The resurrection proves that there is hope and a brilliant Light within you that cannot fail or miss out or even be rejected.

WE know the messages in this book could have been said in other ways. WE honor all messages of Light and truth. This book is set up so there will be no confusion about the principles at hand that can change your life and your planet.

I know Tammy may feel uncomfortable relaying some of these words to you all. WE know she is putting herself out there to display her own fears and illusions. WE know that her journey is yours as well. In spite of herself, she knows this is needed for her and you as well. Tammy is strong-willed, as she knows. WE are asking you to be open to new ways of living. You are worth it. You deserve it.

Tammy, I have asked you before, what is the number one issue or story you have seen over the years?

Hmm...That most people do not love themselves unconditionally.

You may be asking why Tammy would even know that. It is because she has read, coached and talked to over 30,000 clients privately and many thousands more in her days of producing events. WE believe Tammy has had the practice of seeing herself in others and because her clients were not loving themselves unconditionally, neither was she.

I believe that was true.

Loving yourself unconditionally is required for you to receive. In due time means you now know and believe you are worthy of receiving greatness. You know in your heart it is your time to show up. Now, showing up has so many meanings:

A wife in Dakota may be showing up by raising her sister's kids, because she has passed away;

a man in London drives his brother around to show his gifts as a doctor to others in areas where doctors would not work because the money is not there;

a politician has the courage to say the deals on the table are not solving the problems of this world;

a child in Brazil who plays piano after school because he loves it so much;

a priest who became a priest when his family dose not understand his choices;

all of these acts, small or large, are examples of showing up apart from your ego.

In due time is prospering in areas of your lives where your service or talent is beyond you and it touches small groups or masses of people. You are allowing the God talents and abilities to shine through you. You are literally stepping aside to showcase God through you.

Do you get it now? How exciting is that? In spite of what bills need to be paid, in spite of what people are telling you, in spite of your own driven fears, you are showing up anyway. The brilliance of your Self is stepping out. The chances you think you are taking are not chances at all. What it means is that you are changing the force of your direction. You are not allowing the smallness of you or anyone else to dictate your story anymore. How thrilling is that?

Let's talk about Michael Jackson and his talent in music. Thriller was one of those albums WE witnessed Michael create over days and weeks and months. Michael was an open channel to his abilities. Michael had an innocence about his abilities. That is why music came to him so easily. He stepped out of the feedback and the naysayers and the judgment many times to create masterpieces of music that will live many centuries. Michael could tap into that creative frequency, and he knew he was in the brilliance of the Heavens. Michael lived for that. He felt everything. Without going into what broke his soul down, WE want to celebrate his life as one of truth and the talent he displayed over his lifetime. In spite of his upbringing, Michael stepped out on his own and created the most wonderful music.

What you may denounce in yourself is that the talent Michael had, you also have. Your talents and the form they take could also create brilliant work that would hang around for centuries. Just like Einstein and Martin Luther King and many others who live on with their brilliant works, you can create as well. Can you own that yet? Are you even open to the possibilities of your works and talents that are lingering in you just to have a chance to be demonstrated? Due time means you are not believing in anyone else but the God-self in you. You are it. You are a masterpiece waiting to be displayed by yourself. You are not the smallness at all. Your works and talents can pull darkness out of anyone who has given up. Your talents are waiting to be showcased, not just for you, but for many. Your works can change others. Your souls rejoice when you have seen yourselves in others—to wake them up to their journeys. It really is not about you. Do you get that yet? You can help others, but you keep getting in the way with your smallness.

In due time means to go beyond what is happening in your life right now. Wrap your heart around that. If you could change the Light in others to be bright and full of hope again, why would you turn that down? If you could save a child from drowning, could you walk away from that?

Your walk is our walk. It is your turn to shine. What are you going to do with that?

Once you start showing up and living past your stories, others will support you in ways you can't imagine. Light that is brighter than what you can carry, will pull in others like a magnet to be a part of what you are creating with God. Your Source is living through you.

Like Michael Jackson, many others who have lived on your planet to display that Light have shown you what is possible, have died because of their Light and the fears of others who could not understand that Light. Those souls who have died would not change a thing. They did not die in vain; they died in sane and full of Light that still flickers in all of you.

What a soul of Light can do is beyond your planet's evolution. You could not wrap your head around it even if you tried. Look at Oprah and what one soul stood out to do in her life-time. WE are not saying it will always be easy, but a purposeful life changes everyone. It is like a sound wave that tones out lower frequencies and moves like unseen waves, rippling continuously.

You are the Oprah's and the Dali Lamas. You are the Ghandi's and the Martin Luther Kings of your time. Own it. You are the Gods of your time as well. You are it. Do not look around you thinking, *no way*. Yes, way! It is your turn to create from love and Light.

Why do WE believe in you when you do not? Why is that? Please stop playing a victim and start living again.

WE are so passionate about this book being written. WE are patiently waiting as Tammy releases her stories, trying to fix everything. The joy is that she is showing up, maybe not every day, but enough to get this book written. Tammy believes there's got to be another way, because what she knows has not worked. That alone has created this opening for her to play in the brilliant playground of the Universe you all can play in.

Time is a relative term. There is no time where WE are, but there is your time that you created on your planet. The only thing that matters is the aftereffects of your thoughts to yourself and to everyone on your planet. The thoughts you think matter to us because it is all of your thoughts and feelings that create everything.

Join with us in taking the steps toward owning your talents and allowing the juices of God and the forces of the Universe of Light to work through you. Let the force of the God-given abilities work through you. All you have to do is allow and be willing to let God work through you. Can you do that? Give yourself a chance to shine, to win, to live, to serve, to believe again, to rise to the occasion by touching others, to bring change to your planet. WE will continue to hold that vision with you. WE will stand strong and bold to that thought for all of you. There are no exceptions. No one will be left behind. Everyone has the talent of God within him, no matter what the story is. Go be movers and rise—rise above the smallness and witness to each other the stories of hope and joy once and for all.

William, I am really inspired right now.

That was what WE wanted to instill into your soul and heart. Are you committed now?

Totally.

What one person can do to affect millions is worth the display of love and is so contagious and exhilarating for all of you to see. How can that not be exciting and joyous?

You witness such fear on your planet. Why not now choose to witness love and joy?

It is your time—your cycle of life bringing forth hope for all mankind. Breathe in this excitement to the deepest parts of your souls and hearts. This will filter in Light once again to those places you have forgotten.

You are now rising again, and as you rise, you will prosper. You cannot rise without one another. When you rise, you raise everyone, and as you truly prosper, everyone will prosper with you. Go be of good joy today, for it is a wondrous day.

How will you know when you are rising within? As you have followed the last seven chapters and principles, you are already rising within. As you are open to rising, you are automatically internally moving your frequencies to a higher vibration.

Again, what do you want to create in your lives? What would bring you joy, purpose, peace? Answering some deeper questions will release any confusion.

When you can get truly honest with yourselves, you will be able to move mountains and have the ability to see clearer than before. Getting honest about your journey and taking inventory of what is working and what is not working sounds easy enough, but most of you have not been comfortable enough to look within. It is time to do this. Be true again about you. Ask your friends who you trust to tell you what they see in you. Ask just a few friends, and once you have the same answers, you know they are telling you the truth.

What would you change or not change in your life's experience? Would you leave it the way it is? How can you love yourselves and those around you? Telling the truth to yourself is the first step in rising within you. Getting real and honest without judging or hurting yourself or feeling sorry for yourself is the only way. Once you do that, doors will start to open. The rise is such a marvelous gesture to the release of pain. It is so incredible to witness.

If the mirror is showing you that not much is rising or prospering, are you willing to own it? If yes, then take a deep look at things in your life to see what needs to change. Your thoughts for sure—then what? Your inner guidance will show you if you ask to be shown. How eager are you for a life of peace and joy?

It is written that some of you may take longer than others. That is your choice. As this chapter is written, you are opening your souls up to create a rise within. You are deeply asking for another way in your thoughts and your subconscious. What a thrill it is to know your Self again.

Your answers are there if you listen. Listen to them with respect and continue to ask for everyone to win along the way. To set the intention for everyone to win is loving all. WE are expressly worked up with Light and joy for your transformation. WE witness your highs and lows. WE surrender to your thoughts of triumph and wonder as you play in the universal wisdom of the God in all of you.

Give to yourself the truth of who you are, and then turn within to look at what is working and what is not working. Why are you doing what you are doing? Look to see if your actions and thoughts align with love or fear. See what is driving you and motivating you. Are your choices coming from love or fear? Ask for clarity if you do not have it. Ask us for help in all ways. Ask us to show you where to turn, where to look, where to see, where to hear God's voice. Once the clarity is there, look within again for the answers you already know.

As this process is uncovered like a gentle flower with petals that are released, the Light lives within and will pollinate the world, the seeds you plant along the way.

Such incredible truth. It is true that the truth will set you free. It really does. Give yourself the gift to know that.

Joining together is a strong bond, so as WE join with you to know you have risen, it will set us all free once and for all.

When you are ready, WE are moving on to Chapter Nine.

The 9th Principle:
BEYOND THE ILLUSION

Give, Love, Forgive, and Be Compassionate.

Now you are in a space where you can give to others without being exhausted or worn out. The frequency here is derived from such love, logic and truth. Given where you have come from with Chapter One's experience, you will easily be able to be compassionate, because you understand how easy it is to slip into the sleeves of delusion.

This is such an incredible journey and while living Chapter Nine, you are feeling like you are getting a reprieve, a time out. In honesty, you are now at peace again, rejoicing in the realm of Light with less darkness. Your soul is living in moments beyond the illusion. The Light is overpowering the dark. You know and believe the truth again.

Just sighing...out loud.

That is joyous release, is it not?

Yes, it is.

This chapter is all about inner freedom and inner wisdom and inner direction. You have now regained your thoughts and are thinking correctly. The Holy Spirit is living through you like water to a dying plant. You are aligning all of your portals and are lifted past the vast density of your planet. Your soul is singing songs of past and present and future lives, recalibrating your essences and defining anew.

This is the brass ring in the story of the luscious fruits of your labor. The commitment and the consistency of your work is paying off for you. This is your time to shine to be an example for others to see.

To truly give is to give without limits to what your heart and intuition guide you to do. Giving is a vital source for your planet's progression. As you give to other souls, you calibrate their soul along with yours. The gift is what is returned to you. The act of giving releases you both from fear. Giving creates hope, trust and love.

WE challenge you to think of someone or something you feel deeply a part of and want to give to. It could be your time, money, service, an ear for someone to talk to. As you are in the experience of giving, you blast off eons of fear, and you are creating a bond that only God's child can create. Give freely and with gratitude and with joy. Hearts will open up automatically and be replenished.

Let's give examples of what giving is like.

When you have taken on clients even when they could not pay, it is because you knew who they were before they did, and you could not keep yourself from helping them. You cannot wait to work with them because of what is possible.

A man pulls over to help a family stranded on the side of the highway to fix the tire on the car and then follows the family to a gas station before leaving, just to make sure they are ok. The man is leaving without taking anything in return.

How about your hospitals who take in patients without knowing how they are going to pay the bill? Once the patient is released, then the hospital is willing to work with him or her on paying what he owes. That is giving, because the hospital's concern is helping the patient feel better again at the expense of not knowing how things will work out financially.

Your planet has so many great facilities that are put in place to help people, animals, plants and even ocean life. There is so much hope and golden opportunity for all of you. So many volunteer programs are in place and jobs that serve others. It does not matter if you are paid for it or not. What is important is that the intention is to help, to give, to love, to serve, to honor. This comes from a desire to give, to be a part of something bigger than yourself. All of the programs in place can attract the souls they need to continue to thrive.

You created all of those programs and buildings and facilities to have meaning in your lives, to stir the passions of your souls, to brighten your days with miracles and deep connections. All of these are expressions of love, a chance to connect to each other. As you connect to another, you are connecting to yourself as well. You all have so much to learn from each other, to see and feel what it is like to be in someone else's shoes, to know his or her journey and to appreciate who is in front of you.

To give is to also give when someone is not open to it. This may be the hardest to understand—to see others as they really are when they are not acting in a loving way. At some point, they will embrace that love. Yes, and sometimes, the most loving way is to not be around those who are not ready to be loving. But from a distance the best gift you can give from love is to see them happy and that God is with them.

There are some souls on your planet who will not give unless there is something in it for themselves. This is not giving at all. It is manipulation on their part. Most of these souls are aware of what they are doing; however, they are not aware of the principles at hand or even that the Universal Law states that what you give out will come back to you. Do you think it comes back ten-fold?

Not sure.

It is ten-fold and more. So, what you give out comes back to you more than ten-fold—one hundred fold. What are you giving out? Are you helping others? Or are you wanting to see what comes back to you?

There is an old saying that holds so much truth: *If you are seeking love, go be love to others. If you are seeking joy, be joyful to those around you. If you are seeking security in your life, then show others how to be secure within themselves.*

It is like a minister of a church who has to do his lessons and read his scriptures to be on top of his game for his following. What is driving the minister is the ability to deliver a message, but at the same time, he is serving himself along the way.

It is like a nurse who is working long hours and then taking tests and classes to be better for her patients, and in the end, it is allowing her to be better within herself.

As you think of others and how you can be the best you can be at your job, your life, your hobbies, or your playtime, you show up differently. You are serving everyone and everything.

Do you remember when WE said that your energy affects everything around you?

Yes, that was a few chapters back.

Now get this. As you are giving and finding ways to be better at your jobs, lives, hobbies, you vibrate that into the world, so the plants and trees and the air you breathe are better for it too. Everything is connected to you. Your thoughts and feelings touch everything around you, including the people, surroundings, communities and cities, your country, your planet and the galaxies. Can you just picture yourself walking around with everything connected to you? It is like the movie *Contact,* when Jody Foster was talking to her dad and she could touch the air and it reverberated back to her. It really is just like that.

You affect the foods you eat, your seas, land, rocks, air, and the Earth you stand on.

Have you walked into a place and just felt uncomfortable or you immediately got a headache? What do you think that is? It is the result of energies that have been there and are not cleared yet, or could it be the fear of someone's presence that still lingers.

By giving, you would walk into that place and your Light would demolish that darkness into nothing. But until someone does that, it will linger until it is changed. It may take many people to do that, but all that is required is one Light. How bright are you shining right now? How do you think your aura is looking? How clear are you?

As you start to give, you rise easily and your world is better for it. WE will give examples of how powerful you are in giving and what that does for your soul.

You may or may not know about this, but there is a place in Africa that serves the sick men, woman and children who have been long forgotten. There are women who get so sick the families denounce them and put them in shelters, so they are forgotten.

One woman showed up and could not live with knowing this and started this hospital to help those in need, even while their families could not do anything. To this day, that hospital is full of patients and there are lines of people coming in from all over for services and to get help. Lives are reborn because of this one woman. Because of her desire to help, she now has help and a staff who adores her. Do you think she is living a purposeful life? Yes, she is. WE must say it is not always easy and WE do not promise an easy life. WE promise an awakened life full of drive and joy if you want it.

With the rising of female genital mutilation, a hospital is created in Africa to say *no more.* How about the rapes in Kenya, the Somalian famine refugees, the gangs and the criminals? As you see, people are showing up to help those in need. As the dark shows up, the Light shines brighter to turn things around. WE know there are many who are starving from Africa to Syria to Iran, even to your country, America.

Remember, all is given, even in the worst of circumstances. You can create and bring in anyone or anything with a purpose and the Light will triumph all fears. Once you have allowed the Light in all chaos will disappear as peace returns again.

WE know some of the conditions you have been placed in to experience are painful for you, but in retrospect, you can learn through joy, and you can be that soul who shows the way with joy. Sometimes, with hard work and years of struggle, you can learn to thrive again. All it takes is for one soul to say, *no more pain. I do not buy into this story that you are playing out anymore.* That is giving.

WE are elated to see how far you have come. How willing you are to change? Now are you willing to show up to give and live and to step out of your shells to be used by God?

Please do not judge so much the good, the bad, and the painful. What will serve you is to ask *What can I do now, today, this moment?* What has happened cannot be changed.

This leads us into our next topic about forgiving. Can you forgive or do you want to be right? Do you want to say that what happened can never be forgiven? Do you not realize that if you do not forgive yourself or anyone you allowed to hurt you, it will eat you like poison until your body reflects what you are feeling inside? Is it really worth your dying over it? That is what will eventually happen.

Stop the punishment. You are not guilty anymore. Find a way to forgive whomever or whatever it is you are carry around. **Pain stops you. Forgiveness moves you.**

Tammy, tell them the story about Paula and what happened to her.

Ok. When Paula came to me many years ago, she was pretty unhappy and upset because she felt one of her girls who worked for her in the beauty salon she owns used her and then went and opened her own salon not too far away from her.

When I was talking to Paula on the phone, I asked her if she wanted to be right or be happy. Paula wanted to be happy, but she did not have the tools to forgive this girl for what happened. She proceeded to tell me that she told everyone that if she died that this girl was not invited to her funeral. Now Paula was not dying, but she was very angry and could not release it.

Thank God, her brother Roger was also a client of mine, and he recommended that Paula get some coaching sessions.

When we started, Paula was dedicated to doing the work to find her peace again. She knew deep down that she was not thinking right. She was not feeling right either.

As Paula did the forgiveness work, she was feeling so much better. It took about three or four months for her to totally forgive this girl. At that point, our conversations had moved on to other areas of her life.

A few weeks after she had totally forgiven this girl, Paula told me she had to go on a cruise for work and would call me when she got back. I told her to enjoy her trip. A few weeks later, Paula called me with exciting news and was really pleased to tell me that when she got on the ship, this girl was on the same ship with her—the girl who she could not forgive many months before. Paula proceeded to tell me that one night while she was sitting with some other women, this woman approached her, handed her an envelope and told her to not open it until she got off the ship.

Paula told me as soon as she got off the ship, she opened the letter and to her surprise, the girl told her she would not be who she was if it were not for Paula and that she loved and adored her. She told Paula she would never forget her as long as she lives. Paula was so touched by this letter that the two of them made up and are friends again. They may not hang out all of the time, but the miracle happened. All of this happened because Paula was willing to heal her own feelings.

Paula went from not allowing this woman at her funeral to mending their relationship. It was a powerful reunion. Once Paula had forgiven her, it was no accident that this woman happened to be on the same ship as Paula.

This is a true story of how forgiveness heals everyone. The miracle is that Paula was aware she needed help and she knew it was more important to have peace than to be angry. Paula is a kind soul who is giving back to everyone she knows. Now Paula has moments where she may slip at times, but her wisdom and the tools she has, pull her back into truth again.

Take it from Paula. Why would you want to suffer like that? The only thing that Paula did was to accept her responsibility to understand the fact that people do move on and they do not owe you anything but the truth. Paula now does not take it so personally when someone leaves her business. Paula is just a caretaker of a building that serves everyone who comes through it. The Light can shine bright for Paula, and it can for you, too.

If you know you need to forgive, because it just keeps eating at you and you cannot let it go, go into forgiveness, find a technique or ask God to help you. There are many ways to forgive, so look to someone who can show you.

I have to say, William, I so loved working with Paula, and she taught me so much. Her kind heart and commitment to grow spiritually was so inspiring. I loved how she told me the truth about where she was and what she desired.

Yes, Tammy, all of your clients are such gifts for you to see your own reflection of forgiveness.

I know that.

Let's do another example of forgiveness. Tell them the story about your friend Mary and about going to Denny's in the middle of the night.

Do I have to?

Yes, it is a wonderful story.

I had the ability to attract anyone who was an alcoholic into my life—from friends to lovers, you name it. Now, this was before I woke up spiritually. As I was waking up, I lived in Bakersfield, CA, and I did not know many spiritual teachers, so I asked God to bring a teacher in Bakersfield to teach me.

Within the first week, I met Mary. Mary was very spiritual and metaphysical and had been around in the movement since the seventies and worked with a famous teacher.

Mary would tell me story after story about her beliefs, and I could not wrap my thoughts around some of it. I was just starting out on my journey.

Mary was so full of love and cared deeply for me. I adored her, however the one thing that I used to judge about her was that she loved to drink 7 & 7s. The local bar, The Padre, was her hang out. Now I used to drink some too. I just did not understand why I was judging everyone who drank, but it was a deep issue for me.

I remember late one night around 10 pm, Mary called me to pick her up at the bar because she had too many drinks in her. I was at work when she called and did not want her walking home drunk. So on my way home from work, I picked her up at the bar and took her home. Now, I had a small Miata car, a two-seater. You could smell the booze on her, and I was literally disgusted about it. Mary called me on it and said, why are you judging me when you yourself are also a drinker? Mary then wanted me to take her to Denny's so that she could sober up. I agreed to take her, not knowing what was about to happen.

We got to Denny's and we walked inside and sat down at the bar on the barstools. I was watching Mary to make sure she could drink her coffee, and all of a sudden this loud, banging noise was behind us. We both turned around and, to my surprise, there was this homeless man banging against the glass window, drunk as hell.

I looked back at Mary and she said to me, are you ready yet to let go of the judgment about yourself? As I was looking at Mary, I was just starting to get what she was saying, and all of a sudden, the homeless man walked into the restaurant and sat right next to me on the barstool. I had Mary on one side and this homeless man on the other. I knew it was a gift from God and right then and there, I forgave myself.

Mary was laughing so hard, she fell off the bar stool. I forgave myself for who I was inside, an alcoholic from this lifetime and probably past lifetimes too. I now have such compassion for anyone who has addictions in any form. I asked Mary to please forgive me also for judging her, because all she needed was my love, no matter what her choices were. Mary was such a gift and a blessing to know. She always called me on my bull and false beliefs, and I still think of her from time to time.

Yes, Tammy, she was one of many teachers that you have called in to inspire you and to demonstrate truth to you.

Now WE see that you are outdoors writing in front of the most beautiful trees that give clean air to your planet. How pleasant is that?

Very pleasant, I love it.

Forgiveness is like emptying a suitcase that you have been carrying for too long. Lay your suitcases down. Every situation where forgiveness is needed is only an experience where you were in fear, or someone else was. That is it.

You are probably wondering why forgiveness is showing up in Chapter Nine and not in the beginning chapters. That is because once you have embraced the ability to co-create, and once you have your thoughts clearer, you can forgive easier.

Just a summary of what WE mean by this, in Chapter One, you are starting the cycle of finding peace again, to regain your footing. Chapter Two is getting in touch with your true self and being still. Then the third chapter is about rebuilding your worth and the ability to receive love. On to the fourth chapter where you open your channels to release all of your fears. As WE get to the fifth chapter, allowing the truth to flow through you and the divine order to proceed over your journey. And the next chapter is the sixth, you are purified and open to miracles to receive confirmations and bring you into the moment.

The seventh chapter is about owning that you cannot make any mistakes, even if it looks like it. In Chapter Eight you are allowing the Universe to assist you in receiving your aligned callings and gifts as you rise and prosper. Once you are at Chapter Nine, you are more willing and able to just let go of any judgments and pain from your past and the future and of the day. You are aligned to your right-minded thinking.

Now remember this, as these chapters are in sequence, you can arrive at Chapter Nine in just minutes. Do not be under the illusion that this takes a lot of time. It does not. You can arrive at Chapter Nine or for that matter at Chapter Twelve in seconds, minutes, hours, days, months, years, lifetimes. It really is your choice.

WE hear the question you are asking: *Can you do these chapters out of order and still have the same results?*

I don't know.

Yes, you can. For the simplest way to acquire your ownership with God and the Oneness you attain, WE have come up with the principles in the order you can attain them most simply. There is no wrong way to go through this book, no matter what the ego part of your mind is telling you.

Once you have put the principles into practice, you will find out what principles will shift you back to your right mind again. You will be the experience of the principles that move you most. Some days it may Principle One and other days it may be Three or maybe Seven. All of these principles are like hooks of truth, springing you back to your sane minds.

Just listen to your heart and what you feel or what pulls you in. Your style of learning does not matter to us. Just start somewhere, with whatever principle matters to you. As you open up to these principles, you will discover the pull of your soul's requests.

WE are eager to work with all of you. As you are reading the pages in this book, WE are working with you too. You are asking for another way, and WE are responding to you on so many levels.

Yes, you can cycle back and forth, but that does not mean that once you read all of the principles, it works. You have to live the principles. You have to witness the principles working for you in your life. Try the first one and you will be guided to move on to the next one. If the first one does not resonate with you, then go on to Principle Two. You will know from reading the principles where you are at in your present life.

These principles are not complicated—do not let your ego tell you differently. You can move beyond your present and fly with the Heavens at any given moment of the day, even when you are not feeling your best. Let the book read to you. Feel the energy from us, and the spoken words that are written for you. WE will heal your heart and your soul if you let us. What are you willing to do?

The word *love* appears. On your planet, the word has lost its meaning. But the energy of love is beyond your conception. Love is not fixing anyone or rescuing people because you are afraid they are going to hurt themselves. Now WE know you are thinking that, yes, at times you have to go help someone because she forgot to love herself. Or you need to call 911 because maybe someone is about to hurt himself. That is understandable.

What is not understandable is when you feel you need to rescue someone and fix his problems because you believe in your mind he cannot take care of himself out of fear. Watch your actions. Are you coming from love or fear? It really is all energy.

What do you mean by this, William?

Every action you take comes from one of two energies—one of love or of fear. Period.

Ok.

Say, for instance, you bought someone a gift, but the energy you feel around it was fear. Do you think they are going to appreciate it?

No.

Yes, they will not appreciate it at all. When you build a cycle of giving from fear, it only generates results of fear, no matter what form your giving takes.

I get this more than you know.

So does everyone else reading this book. When was the last time you gave a gift or something and you knew deep down it was totally from love? Take a moment before you give anything and ask yourself if you are truly giving from love or fear.

Tammy, tell the story about the wedding your friend gave for her daughter. This is an example of giving from fear and not love.

A friend of mine, I am going to call her Joanne, was going to pay for her daughter's wedding. Joanne and her husband were so eager to help their daughter.

What happened was that Joanne's daughter came to her and her husband to say they were not good parents and that they owed *her the biggest wedding ever. When I talked to Joanne after the wedding, Joanne was so hurt and she had felt much guilt about what her daughter had told her and her husband. Instead of working things out with their daughter, Joanne and her husband paid for a huge wedding. I think they spent over $60,000.*

After the wedding was over and their daughter was on her honeymoon—which Joanne and her husband paid for—Joanne called me crying because her daughter was complaining that the wedding was not as good as she had hoped for.

I felt so much for Joanne and her husband to have to go through this.

Tammy, what is important to see is that Joanne and her husband operated from fear, guilt, shame and that energy did not serve Joanne or her husband or even her daughter. It is not about all that you do, it is about the energy it comes from—love or fear. Your actions can come from love always.

What do you think Joanne and her husband should have done when her daughter came to her with her feelings?

Worked out what was happening. Not agree to what she wanted.

Joanne and her husband should have talked to her and asked to work things out between themselves or hired a professional, not acted so quickly in trying to buy love. You cannot buy love. You cannot earn it. You cannot fix it. You cannot bargain for it. Most people on your planet, for example, will overcompensate when they feel guilty or ashamed of their own actions. What do you think needs to happen?

Forgiveness.

Yes, and once you have done that, your actions will come from love. Holding anyone back in fear because you think it is love creates a dependency. To try to overcompensate to anyone because of your fears or someone else's fears breaks the golden rule of what love is.

Love is love, a feeling of pure joy and an expression of Oneness, a connection that all parties are feeling. When you are loving, the other parties involved feel the same thing. It is an experience where the gift is already given. All parties work together, agreeing so everyone is happy. Do you think your parties in government are coming from love?

Not at all.

Yes, both parties want to win, but in the end, no one wins. If you cannot agree to work together, then you will destroy the parties and separate into even more divided groups. That is what is happening. Is it not?

Yes, it is.

In moments that can be healed, love is simple and yet complicated for you to demonstrate.

So how can we love ourselves and others more?

Great question. The way to love yourself is to appreciate yourself and others; to fully accept who you are, no matter what flaws you think you have; to accept that first you incarnated on your planet; to accept your journey as an experience to meet some incredible souls; to appreciate what you are—a soul that lives from love, joy, laughter, innocence. What it comes down to is embracing your body, soul, mind, etheric being. To love does not mean only conditional love either. To love is to love without limits. Love is loving, no matter what your past and present are. Love is saying, *I do not have to do anything more but to embrace myself as I am.* Be your own best friend. What are your feelings about yourself? If your feelings are not loving, look at that and how you can see yourself differently.

The more you come from loving yourself, the more you can love others. Be kind to yourself. Love is not the sensation you feel from another. Love is deeply appreciating another's goodness and your own. Love is a choice. The sensation is not the love, but the effects of a lesson to learn. The more intense the connection, the more the lesson to be learned. Love is content and not the form.

Yes, WE know your movies display moments of passion and the desire to be with another. There is nothing wrong with wanting to be with another soul, body and mind. The passion that is mixed with another person or a pursuit of trying to create love is a beautiful thing. To be passionate about connecting and creating is love expressing through you. But do not get confused about the feeling of the sensation and passion. They are two completely different experiences.

As WE talk about love, the passion that derives from the love is like the topping of a root beer float. When you are passionate about anything, the love was present first. Passion is very intoxicating and can stir many souls to muster from floors of hell to the springs of joy, to follow the soul who is passionate.

What do you think sells your products and all of your devices?

Do tell, William.

Most of the products sold in your time and all time have passionate souls who stand behind their products. Passion sells. You can sell anything from love. Remember that passion is the result of love.

I have not thought of it that way before.

Find your passions and know that the love was there way before you discovered what you loved to do.

Continuing on with love, do you believe that animals feel love?

Yes, I do.

Animals vibrate in a frequency just like humans, and the love that comes from animals can be just like humans—very loving and sometimes not very loving.

The difference between humans and animals, besides the obvious, is that animals vibrate higher than humans. Their senses are more open. Animals have the ability to let go of things easier because of where they vibrate. Now from time to time, you will understand that an animal has been hurt way too many times and cannot get past it until an animal expert steps in.

Love comes in all forms: people, animals, your calling, your homes, your communities, churches, your country and even your planet. You can love many people, places and things.

As WE wind down the love factor and all of its attributes without the hype or the sales pitch, WE advise just to start on yourself. Look within and see the parts of you that you love and acknowledge that. One of the easiest ways to enjoy love around you, besides bringing in souls who care for and love you, is to love the space you occupy. Your homes should have a loving energy that you cannot wait to stay in. When you come home from a day's work, you should be looking forward to being in your home, your space.

As you feed love to yourself, it feeds your soul's bank account. You cannot give from an empty vessel. Loving yourself is looking around and being honest enough to say what is feeding you from love and what is not.

Love is in all of your cultures and spreads over all of your continents and is part of all of your lives. That love is within every soul that wants to express itself truly with another. You were never made to be separate. To join with another requires joining together. Love is the springboard to hope and faith. Love dispels all illusions. When you come from love, you create miracles. When you know you are love, you are the miracle. Where do you want to come from? Stop thinking about how your world ticks and seek within the ticking of your spirit. Connect with the truth within.

Love is felt not by words but by feelings, the connections you have with another or group. Love holds no bounds. Love has patience and holds no grievances.

Who are you not loving on this day as you read this? What part of love are you holding back? The fear you carry because of past hurts is causing you more hurt when you hide from love or are too afraid to feel it again.

Align your thoughts back to love. Think of how you felt the last time you even felt love. How happy were you then? That is because you were open to expressing your true self. Love is your true self. Love stays open as you stay open to it. It is your choice always. If you are not feeling it, change it.

WE witness so many swirls of hate that you may call love. What is love has no demands or expressions of shame or guilt. Consider how you would like to be treated from a place of innocence. Treating others with kindness and high regard is rejoicing with love. Your responses and your actions express your love or your fears over and over.

Watch so many souls who rebound back from the darkness to be redeemed, and many accolades are given. Redemption is the rubber band symbolically coming back to its original form. All of you are redeemable, no matter what your story was and no matter how far down the hole you went. Would you not welcome a brother or sister who was lost for a while? Would you not give them rest and food and shelter? Would you not give them a safe place to be? Or would you rub the salt in their wounds and kick them to the curb? Some of you have done that and some of you have not. How would you like to be treated? Give what you desire to another. Give from love, and as you do, the compassionate spirit you are will swim in glory.

Your true selves want to share and to give glory to others and most of all to yourselves. Coming into compassion shows that you all could be walking in their shoes, that everyone is vulnerable to what the ego can do. You succumb to knowing your walk is your sister's or brother's. You look at the glory and the kindness of what is present in your experience. You have the compassion to refrain from beating yourselves up, or anyone else. You have reverence for what others are going through.

You start to see the common denominator in each other. Compassion creates a desire to alleviate any thought of suffering for another or for yourself. You become empathetic to others' journeys, and while you share in their stories, you actually are reducing their fears and yours at the same time. Compassion is a part of love that expresses an equal partnership with each other. It denies that any separation ever occurred. It is as if you are walking on water like

Jesus did, but you are showing the beauty and the transference from the compassion back to love again.

Here is a story from not too long ago about a wonderful soul who indeed lost its way on the journey, and the recovery of love from another, and how it allowed the redemption to happen.

Many, many years ago, there was this wonderful man who loved his family. He was raised by a wonderful mother and father who adored him. Let's call him Samuel. While Samuel was raised by his mother and father, he had such a curiosity about life even as a small boy. Samuel had to be watched in order to not disturb the day's activities. As Samuel grew into a young man of twenty-two, he started to believe that his family did not understand him because Samuel felt so different. One night, Samuel planned to leave in the middle of the night without telling anyone where he was going. Once the mother and father woke up to find Samuel gone without note or warning, they were heartbroken.

Many years passed, and as Samuel was experiencing the world and learning many lessons of life, Samuel's mother and father held him in high regard and set a plate and fork at their table every night. Samuel's parents were very compassionate about what had happened to the point they were not even angry about what Samuel did. They felt it was his choice to leave and knew the things that Samuel needed to learn could not come completely from them or their small town.

Samuel's parents did not think Samuel owed them anything. They were steadfast in their hopes that one day Samuel would return, even if it were just for a visit. Samuel's parents knew that they, too, had to learn their lessons and that each soul has a journey of its own. More years went by and, yes, they deeply missed their son. One day more than five years later, there was knock on the door. Samuel's mother opened the door and, to her amazement, she saw Samuel again with a beard, and wife and child.

As Samuel and his parents came together that night with extra plates around the table, all the parents wanted to know was what he had done and what he learned from his travels. The love and compassion were present. The love they had for their son was without guilt or suffering. They just had a longing to see their son again. As the son told them of his travels and his journey and why he felt he had to leave, the family cried together and embraced each other.

It is noteworthy that WE did change the name from Joseph to Samuel, Jesus' dad with mother Mary. WE wanted to share the story of redemption and glory and what love and compassion can do. Joseph knew deeply that his parents would receive him in love and would rejoice in his journey. This is a story of love and redemption and what miracles can do. Do you think that Joseph and Mary were the only ones who believed and created miracles? Mary's and Joseph's upbringing demonstrated such love and compassion, the union that held Mary and Joseph in honor. That is why Jesus was born to them. God knew they could handle it without the fear of themselves or others.

What is demonstrating in your families? How are you holding everyone up? Do you believe in them and have compassion for their journeys? Even if their journey is different from yours? Even if maybe their beliefs are different? Give wonder to others and see them as brave beings on the mission to discover themselves. The props and the people who show up are all gifts.

Remember all of the wonderful souls who raised their hands to come into your journey and were eager to help you and you help them to remember who they are. Compassion heals and connects you to others. So what if you come from different cultures and different beliefs? WE all require love.

Go be compassionate today and treat others the way you wish to be treated. Live with love in your heart. Display your soul's joy to others, no longer needing to hide. As you rise, you bring others with you.

Moving on to Chapter Ten. You compassionate souls, WE see you and feel your love pouring out.

Remembering One, Once Again

The 10th Principle:
ERASING THE VEIL

Open your eyes to see that we are all connected.

Erasing the veil is not like the veil or "caul" on a new-born baby. It can be similar in nature to you carrying an invisible cover over your bodies that cannot be seen by you or anyone else. As the veil is lifted that cover is removed completely in an etheric realm.

Let's start by explaining the caul or the rare occurrence of a baby being born with a caul or amniotic sac around the baby's head like a helmet that can be removed. As in your world, it represents some special gifts or psychic powers. But in truth, it does not define that. All of you possess psychic abilities. No one is special.

From the title *Erasing the Veil*, as you come into Principle Ten, you will discover the feeling and the instinct that you are connected not just to people but to everything around you. You will start to feel a sensation of sorts that you are more than your own body—that you are One with everything. With this occurrence you will embark on a journey with renewed joy and hope, because you are now feeling what it means to be One with everything. This may appear in a meditation, or when you are standing on the corner waiting for a bus to show up, or even when you are sleeping. This connection will overwhelm you with such wonder and a remembrance of who you really are—Oneness with all that is.

You may be thinking, *I do not feel this connection yet.* You will. You can ask to feel the connection to others as you move in and out of your day. Just the thought that you now know and are willing to believe that you are connected creates the experience. Feel beyond your bodies.

Erasing the veil is crucial for joining everyone together. Once you have taken ownership to the Oneness energy, the ego has vanished completely in those moments or seconds. You can call it whatever you want. Erase your thoughts of separation or even feelings that you are separate. Let go of the thought that no one can feel or sense what you are thinking. There are no private thoughts. What you think and feel, others can feel and think it too.

You may be asking, *how can I get to the point where the veil is erased?* By first owning that you are not separate and by celebrating that you are not alone. By asking to feel what it feels like to be connected to everyone. By doing meditations that have you connected to others in meditation. By connecting to the plants and trees, to the oceans, to the sky, and to beautiful souls you see every day. The way to connect is to appreciate what's in front of you. To see the beauty and the worth in all people, places, things, for they all are a part of you.

How do you think long distance healing occurs? Do you think that psychic readings can be done over oceans and continents? It is because there is no separation from anyone. No matter how shut down someone may be, you can still feel that soul. You can also connect to the angels in Heaven, loved ones who have passed on. You can tap into the God energy and even to your Higher Self. This is also why thoughts are so, so powerful. When you want to heal others, whether in spirit or Earthbound, your thoughts of love can heal them and you as well. Seeing someone completely well and joyful is true healing. Letting go of any story of sickness that created the disbelief in wholeness is the resurrection that will heal everyone on your planet. Even if you are just healing one soul it affects everyone.

William, can we heal those who have crossed over too?

Yes Tammy, as you have many times. You have crossed over many who did not feel they deserved the Light. You helped those who wanted to talk to their mothers or fathers or family members to ask for forgiveness, to heal each other. You were the conduit for that, and so is everyone else. As you are open to the truth, it will appear, but not in a box and not structured to fit into your beliefs. Open your beliefs beyond what you think you know is also a state of feeling the oneness.

Sounds like a lot. I bet there are so many beliefs of truth we cannot tap into.

Yes, there are many beliefs that your world has not discovered yet. As you open that Pandora's box and let it lay down flat without bounds, WE can work with you. WE are here to hold you sacred and to share the Golden Light of truth with you. Your world as you know it needs a new way of understanding. WE know WE keep telling you that, but it is true. You are not the world you live in. That, by definition, is a box and a trap in itself.

What you think of as truth is only your life's worldly experience. Your worldly experience is only a small fraction of what the truth is. Dare to ask what the truth is here. Do not get tied up in knots over the props and the small lies your ego tells you.

Lifting the veil or erasing the veil is key to seeing what is true. You are the creator of your world. You created the sun and the rain and the trees on your planet. WE know the Bible says God created the Earth. What God created was you. You are Earth.

Some may argue with this.

Maybe they will and maybe they won't. What is true is that God is love and nothing else. God does not see pain or sin. God only sees Light and love. The rest you created with the ego.

Once that part of you releases the veil, the ego does not have a chance.

Why is that?

Once you are aware and are experiencing the connection with others, you will feel yourself in everyone you meet or see. Your life will be completely different. You will love others more because you will feel they are you.

How many people have done this, William?

Many, and more are coming into knowing the truth.

As you discover this ability within yourself, WE are holding the faith that you can sustain it longer to see and witness the feelings of others, to send love and joy and hope, as you feel the connections.

What do you think a singer on stage feels?

The audience.

Yes, and that is a basic way of understanding this. The singer can feel what a crowd feels. Also the audience can feel what the singer is feeling too. If the audience is sending love to the singer on stage, the singer can feel this and it ricochets back and forth empowering everyone in the room. If the audience is not loving, the singer can feel this as well. What is so important to know, is that in a room with thousands of people, it requires only one soul to change to love to change the whole room back to love again. How do you think the singer feels when they are surrounded by love?

Very empowered.

Yes, the singer feels empowered, euphoric, alive and full of such love. It may look like she is addicted to it, but she is not. She is now in a place within her that has felt what love is.

That sounds like such a contradiction to what you said love was.

Yes, WE know that may sound that way. To clarify, love is appreciation, admiration. The energy of love is powerful and goes through your whole being, soul, spirit, body, mind. That is what the audience is giving to the singer on stage.

The aftereffect of love is felt. That is the result of the love. Euphoria is felt and a haze appears that makes you feel like you are not there, but you are. When two people or more are connected, you feel more than yourself.

You are feeling full of love and expressing energy that has nothing to do with your body. It has everything to do with your soul and spirit delivering energies of love. You can actually be with someone and not even feel your own body. You can be completely taken over with the feeling that there is no time or space because you are an open energy of complete love.

Have you not felt that at times in your life?

Yes, I have. Especially when I have spoken in front of groups of people. I cannot feel anything not even my body. I remember once when I was doing a group reading and my black velour pants I had on were shedding from the energy coming from me and the energy in the room. My friend, Kathy thought there were ants on the floor surrounding me like a puddle but come to find out it was from my pants! We laughed about that for days. Yes, I still had my pants on and by looking at my pants they looked fine.

Tammy that is a wonderful story to tell a grand mixture of love flowing back and forth between the audience and you, which is also lifting the veil. Lifting the veil is beyond your body, your ego. Many of you lift the veil and are not even aware of it. Another example is a furniture salesman who knows his products so passionately when he is trying to sell or explain why you should buy them. He is lifting the veil because he is immersed in his knowing and sharing with another. You cannot help but feel what he is telling you.

To lift the veil is to express love beyond yourself and your ego. Lifting the veil is an automatic connection between you and everything in and around you and everything not around you.

What?

When the veil is lifted, you are connected to everything seen and not seen. You are open to all of God's glory and the presence of Oneness. You are operating in your right mind. You are living the right mind, expressing through you.

Sounds wonderful.

It is. The more you operate from this space, the more joy and love is expressed. When you are vibrating from this place, many souls and lives are transformed. You release all into the Light in an instant.

Lifting or erasing the veil is an aftermath of your thoughts in alignment with the Holy Spirit, God. It is an incredible expression of your true Self.

The reason WE have put this into a principle is because the more often you experience this state of mind, your ego cannot change your experience. You are more convinced that there is more going on past your worldly experiences. You will be changed completely. Remember, experience is wisdom.

Talking spiritually is one thing, but living spiritually is to emend your soul and dip into those corners of your soul in a way unlike any other. As you dip your soul into the comfortable and uncomfortable parts that you are aware and not aware of, your Self relinquishes the dark and light pockets shimmer into what is real, releasing what is not real. But as the veil is lifted, truth can only be known through your experience that everything is connected.

WE see your journeys full of life and hope, and WE know that your expression of love through lifting the veil is a sure way back home again. Your truth is everyone's truth. Everyone, even if he or she does not own it yet, wants the truth.

The veil is seen as the Gate of Heaven, opening to your purpose, to your heart, and to your spirit. All illusions are shattered as the veil is lifted.

As the veil is lifted, you realize the world you believed in is not true. Second, you will experience that you really are not a body, you are more than that. You experience the spirit of yourself as you are, still capable of feeling and thinking. You also are aware that you do not have to die to do this. You can live this experience as a living being. You are now conscious and a part of everything else that is conscious.

How can you lift the veil?

You can lift it by personal events in your life or by direct realization.

You can go through a near-death experience, which will cause the veil to lift, or you could be in a situation in your life that calls for assistance from the angels and guides who intervene in your calling for help. You may or may not recall the lifting of the veil.

The lifting of the veil happens almost every night when you sleep and you are in the alpha-beta levels in your brain. The veil is set aside as you are assisted in your dreamtime to heal or receive guidance. Dreams are very important messages on your journey. The more you use a dream journal, the more you create that muscle to assist you.

One other way is through direct realization by requesting that the veil be lifted by daily affirmations or intentions and prayer. Also the veil is lifted in mediation because in mediation you are at a higher frequency.

You may be asking if this can hurt you in any way as you lift your veil. No, you cannot be hurt in anyway. At the point that the veil is lifted, you are vibrating from a place in which no density of darkness can live. You are free of the illusions of your worldly pains and of your own.

Sounds wonderful. Lift my veil. Sounds like, ring my bell, *a song from many years ago.*

Funny. You can exercise your Divine Being with others. We as one and many are Elohim, the plural name for God. You are God, expressing as a collective consciousness with others, without time or space. You can see what is really going on. It is as if you were covered before the veil was lifted. Your awareness is completely changed, your experiences have expanded to another way of living.

Take the time to Google "lifting the veil," and you will see thousands and thousands of interpretations of the meaning. There is a simple answer to this. Lifting the veil is lifting what is not true anymore. It is a symbolic cover no longer needed. You no longer desire to think of this world. Your thoughts are coming from truth.

There is no fear in seeing the truth or feeling it. It is an experience like no other, and you feel love like you have never felt before. Allow yourself to be open to experience the connection with others.

I know you are writing a lot of different meanings about the veil and it sounds repetitious. Is there a reason for this?

Yes, WE know that the way you remember things is by repeating them, sometimes over and over again with the same message in mind. Your Course in Miracles does this very well.

Your limited mind is now expanding apart from what you see from day to day. You are starting to understand that to have another way of living means thinking and seeing things differently. That means beyond your world, past your everyday thoughts. It sounds so foreign, and it is. But as soon as you start getting the truth, the spirit and soul of you will ring true to their truth as if your past lives step in to greet you, like a lost friend who has returned.

What will appear is a knowing that you were really caught up in the dream or the false movie that has been playing. The only thing that is real is beyond what you can see right in front of you. Can you get the concept that your props—all of them—mean nothing? Only the thoughts about them retain the truth if you will let them without any judgment.

The barrier the ego holds right up to your face is that you are so concerned about the picture frame and not the picture in the frame. WE know you are ready to see the picture and not the props. Many have checked in to see the movie and have not left the theater yet. It is time to stop the movie and to see what is really happening. Your actions should be from what is next in truth and not what is next in the illusion.

This principle is simple and the only thing that could help your request to lift the veil is the discovery of truth. You do not have to be afraid of the unknown, because as soon as you are released from the drapes of darkness, the Light shimmers in.

Can you oblige your right mind to see and feel the presence of God?

Yes, we are ready, William.

Now you are truly ringing your bell and lifting your veil at the same time.

Funny, William.

I thought you would like that.

I do.

Moving onto Principle Eleven, WE will show that this principle is self-explanatory and simple.

The 11ᵗʰ Principle:
CAPTURING THE ONENESS

Open your mind to experience the Oneness.

To capture the Oneness is to grasp that we are really all One and not separate from each other, even when your bodies say, *you are over there and I am over here.* The Oneness is a literal statement that is beyond your conception by yourself. Oneness is a fact or state of being unified or whole though composed of two or more parts, your identity in harmony with someone or something.

To truly capture the Oneness is to ask and allow your God-Source energy to run through your spirit, your mental and physical and your etheric well-being. Once you have given access to the Holy Spirit to enter into all parts of you, then you will experience the Oneness.

Once you have the experience of Oneness, you will have experienced God's glory dissolving your illusions. Your experience will shatter any false thinking that you believed you were ever separate. You are now having an experience of Oneness and your perceptions are now transformed completely.

You will regain a sense of purpose and Divine Presence of unity like no other. It is one thing to know that you are not separate, but until you have an experience to show you the belief that you are One with everyone and everything, you will not dispel the illusion at all. Your world keeps showing you the false sense of what the ego's reality is. It is a dream that is not real.

Your ego will convince you in any way it can that there should be fear in even thinking of thinking differently. The ego part of you will even convince you that there should be fear in letting go of the control. The ego convinces you that you have control, when in reality, you have no control. You are either operating from fear or from love at all times. Your thoughts either come from fear or love every second of the day.

Who is winning in your thoughts? To experience the Oneness is a golden opportunity to witness how disillusioned you really are. Once you have experienced even for just a brief moment what Oneness is, you will never be the same. You will not only realize that you are connected to everything and everyone, but you will also realize that your thoughts were not right before, and now you are more aware and alert of what the truth is. You will also experience a deep sense of peace and a belonging.

The ego part of you cannot dispute this or put you back in your wrong mind. A preacher or friend or a book can tell you over and over again that you are not separate, but it does not register because you have not had the experience to own Oneness for yourself.

When you experience the Oneness, you go beyond your mind. You open your soul and your chakras to a portal that aligns you to All That Is. You are free of body and lower-level thoughts. You are One with everything and everyone. It is a feeling like nothing you know of in your world. Are you ready to experience this?

Yes, William. I know we all want to experience the Oneness.

Tammy, tell them about one of your friends who was explaining a relationship she was going through that you could relate to.

Ok , William. Wow, that was many, many years ago. I had walked into a store and Samantha saw me coming in and came right up to me. She was upset and wanted to explain to me what was going on with her and her partner. They were having problems in their relationship. As soon as the details of the story were coming out of her mouth, I could relate to each word and how she was feeling. I knew in my own life, ten years prior, that I had similar issues in a relationship. Within minutes of Samantha talking to me, I felt the connection. I could see myself in her completely as if we were one. It was a timeless moment. We both knew that we were experiencing a miracle. We had such compassion for each other and the tears started running down both of our faces. It was as if her story were my story. She realized she was too hard on herself and vowed to let go of the hurt she was feeling. We both had a light-bulb moment, knowing that the problems were never bigger than the solution. We knew it was a moment to cherish and to appreciate. I have never forgotten it.

As you all open yourselves up to the connection that you are one with everything you will want to experience this more often than not. You will regain your ability to see and feel and believe in new ways of being, living, breathing.

You will not want to hurt another. You will want the best for all souls and mankind. You will want the best vibration where you walk and live. You will know the deepest meaning of how your vibration touches and feeds in and out with others around you and on your planet. One soul can change your existence and how you all function. Where is the possibility of you living in connection with others? The possibilities are all around you constantly. Every experience is a possibility to connect and to heal each other. That is what the source of your spirits desire to do.

The way to open your minds is to agree to be open to the thoughts that you are connected to everything and everyone. Asking your God-Source and Higher Self to allow an experience of Oneness is all that is needed. It is not complicated to bring in. Questioning your existence without fear is also an opening for truth to enter. To realize all that you know is backwards to what the truth is, also is a way to open yourself up to experiencing the Oneness.

The statement, *as you give, you give to yourself,* is so elementary and a fact of your life forces. What you give another you give to yourself.

Tammy is asking in her head, *Do our ancestors create miracles for us? Has the work of our beloveds affected our journeys too?*

Yes, because there is only one of you here to begin with. What another does, as an ancestor or a fellow soul on his or her own journey, affects everyone and everything. So all that has happened in the history books to those stories you will never hear about has and will continue to affect your lives too. What can make the difference on your soul's journey is to be alert and conscious of your journey. Even a kind act, gesture or thought will uplift all of you.

Capturing the Oneness is not just feeling the Oneness, but asking yourself, *What can I do for my fellow brother or sister? What would I like to see happen? How can I treat that stranger with love and harmony?*

Capturing the Oneness is going past your life to give to another, letting go of any thoughts of what you are getting out of it, or how you can get what you need in the equation.

The Oneness is unifying everyone in harmony all together—listening to the stories of 9/11 on TV about how everyone came together for days and weeks after the event took place. There were no concerns about their stories, their skin colors, their orientations, or whether they were poor or rich. Everyone reached out to each other and did not have any second thoughts about why they were doing it. Everyone came together to heal and to recover from a dark event. WE would like to see you all getting together to think of another without needing a dark event to create it.

How can you open to your Oneness and create actions that demonstrate it? What is so wonderful about helping others is that it takes you out of your stories and thoughts of pain to stand up in Light for something or someone else.

Oneness is asking, how can you serve your soul and someone else's? How can you live in giving and receiving love? How can you love in living with others? How can you share your talents and traits with someone else? Who are you lifting up besides yourself? As you have moved into Chapter Eleven, now is the time to show up differently with others. It is living past yourself and creating something bigger than you. You now realize that no one can hurt you or take anything away from you.

Why not believe in the Oneness—not just in yourself but in others? Let your life be an example of your Oneness. Let your actions show you how others are responding to your giving. Go give and live. See what the miracles can do for all. You are witnessing so many people coming in and out of your lives to show you how you can give back. The act of giving is a sign that you are in agreement that you are not the only one, that what you give you are giving right back to yourself.

WE know that your remarks will be that maybe not so many people are thinking of others on your planet. To your surprise, many people are thinking of others; however, WE would like to see more people thinking of others. Tammy, WE see your readings, your coaching sessions and your workshops working beautifully because of the joining of all energies involved. When you join with another, it becomes intimate. Everything you say or do becomes intimate. That is how all of you can tell you are connecting. It is not about the form of how close you are in body to another. The intimacy is an open invitation between all parties involved, and the form is powerless because it does not matter. You stepped out of your ego to help another and got out of your own way. You are the souls that desire the connections. Connecting is the ability to communicate love without fear. WE have such hope and joy because you would not be reading this book if you did not request another way.

Give yourself permission to let others join with you. You are joined with so many wise and incredible souls. You all came in at exactly the right time designed by Divine Order in your lifetimes. You also agreed to incarnate with all of the billions of souls on your planet.

Your journey is rich and full of such love and a deep vastness that goes past your souls and past your bodies. Your journey is connected not just to other souls on your planet, but also to the heavens and the oceans. Your spiritual cord is connected to All That Is.

You have the free will and the ability to tap into your God-Source energies from the Holy Spirit to the saints in Heaven who live inside you. WE are not far away. The Heavens are within you at all times. WE are within you as well. Your soul's spirit springs forth your inheritance from all who ever lived and who will live throughout eternity.

You can speak and connect to your guides, angels and all of those who lived before you and are living now. What a concept that you can talk to whomever you want to at any time of the day or night. You can speak to God, to your all-knowing, loving Higher Self. You can connect beyond your planet to the wisdom of the Gods of Gods, the Council of Twelve, the White Brotherhood, Jesus, whomever you would like to speak to.

You can talk to your ancestors and find out anything you want to know. Get past the illusion that you can only connect to what you can see. That is dimming your existence. Give God and your soul's evolution a chance to open past the boxes you created. Open up to other ways of living. Being connected to Oneness is also being open to the unseen forces that are there to help and deliver you from the fears of your world.

Capturing the Oneness is the Oneness of everything and everyone. To own that you do not have clue or even a concept of what this is will start to open the doors that shield you from what is possible. You open to the Oneness in dreamtime more than you do in the daylight. Why not say, *I am willing to vacillate between the worlds of God's wisdom and the function of living on planet Earth?* This will deliver you from your solo journey to a soul journey full of riches on so many levels.

Symbolically, WE are on bended knee, holding a helping hand out for you. This is the Oneness WE are giving to you. Remember, you cannot do this by yourself. You will not survive alone on your planet without much pain. Once you realize this, you will see that WE are here waiting to assist you. With only a willingness or a request, WE come running to help you. You are the Oneness that opens the chorus to sing songs you have forgotten. Your brilliance is singing past the smallness of your worldly beliefs. Go question our request—just one golden opportunity to bring in more than your soul, to pour out the greatness within.

William, you are a real poet.

Tammy you are all poets, painters, singers, actors, writers, speakers. You have the same talents that WE do. You just have forgotten, or you do not believe it. Stop doubting who you are. Say, *No more lies to who I thought I was.* Your endings and your beginnings are also illusions, because you are more than all the beginnings and endings of your lives.

You are shimmering lights that burn deep flickers into others. Your soul thrives for moments of flickers. Why are you holding back from the vastness of who you are? All the skies of Light and stars and all of the Earth's core cannot even measure up to the millions of Lights that twinkle inside of you. No measuring tape could be used to measure your Light force. But as long as you have forgotten this, you cannot dip into it at the levels you are capable of. WE are here to remind you of this. Each of you has the same vastness within.

All it takes is a decision to say, *I am more than I know and believe, and I am now willing and ready to reach in and to open up to it.*

You are the hope and the Light of your world. How does that feel to you?

William, with the way you are writing, I feel like I am floating into my deepness, and I am open, along with everyone else reading this, to be One with everything and everyone.

WE are smiling with joy as you surrender and are open to those parts of your Light you have not even tapped into. Swim with us in spirit and dance with us as WE dance a new dance; you now flow freely with the energies of life. You are now living and loving with us as WE ask for another way of being together.

You can create Oneness with your oceans, trees, plants and animals. You can create Oneness with a candle light next to your night stand. You can create Oneness with words of hope and songs that are sung with deep reverence. You can create Oneness with just a feeling of love and wonder. You can create Oneness with a common thread that will weave you both hope and joy.

As WE all do this together, WE are now opening new dimensions and portals that will raise us all above any need for madness or sadness. Dare to ask for another way of living. Dare to walk past any separate thoughts that no longer bind you or your brothers or sisters. You are all children of God and are also souls that are serving each other.

Capturing the Oneness is the ascension process that is not an event, but rather a momentum. It is a shift in awareness and a shift in perception of the soul, a shift in vibration and a shift in alignment with who one truly is.

You realize you are creating all that is a part of all creation and that your thoughts are part of all thoughts on your planet and all thoughts not of your planet. As you know, the power to co-create and to open to your Oneness creates new realities not of your world.

What takes place as you experience Oneness is that your perception of self and the world around you become intertwined. You are actually feeling the process of life and how it lives. You come together with others singing to an instrument. As a living instrument, you are playing different notes together, making the most beautiful music. The voices and sounds of your Oneness are so harmonic that they blend like angels singing in the soul.

As you are One with everything and everyone, your heart opens completely to the gratitude and compassion for others because you feel they are you. You become aware that the God you seek is living in your heart—not far away from you but within your heart center. You feel like you have arrived to what has been there all the time.

You will be carried past your thoughts and your visual perceptions to a place of being-ness that is the embodiment of timelessness.

Sounds so easy and beautiful. Why is it so hard for us to do?

Because of your daily life. You create continuous traps to hold you down. You are trapped in fears that need not be.

But William, so many people are trying to feed and take care of themselves.

Yes, WE see that. As you open to your Oneness and who you are inside, that will become your reservoir of monies beyond what you have on your own. Your wealth is internal and that river of supply is endless if you dare to tap into it.

I dare for so many reasons. I hold the thought that so many others do too.

Yes, and you will be given all from that place within. Believe in you and the Oneness and the miracles will bounce off you like drops of rain. The drought that you see in your cities is symbolic of your own drought within you. The floods you also see in your cities are your own floods within, because your inner faucets have been turned on full blast. You are finding new ways of being. A steady, consistent flow of love and truth is all you need. You cannot miss the mark of receiving God's intervention. You are entitled to it. You are all Gods bearing witness to your inner callings.

The Oneness is just a step into the principles beforehand. Just allow and receive. It's time. Do you agree? Inside of your spirits, you are all alike, no different. Only on the outside are you different, which is an ego device to confuse you. What you have inside is the same that everyone else has. The only other thing that can create confusion is your thoughts. Your thoughts can hinder or deliver you. Oneness delivers completely.

Open your minds to the thought that you are One with everything and everyone, and as soon as you do, the experience will slip into your make-up and free you of false stories.

Could you be the answer you are waiting for? Absolutely you are. Own your perfection and your Light as WE see it in you.

As your day unfolds, see everyone as Lights and feel the connections between you and others. Start with that exercise and watch what happens.

Oneness is. Oneness is all, Oneness is and Oneness will always be forever, no matter what form you create from your ego. Oneness delivers everyone.

On to Chapter Twelve.

Remembering One, Once Again

The 12th Principle:
RETURNING HOME TO ALL THAT IS

**When we no longer need the separation,
we will truly be One again.**

What do you think home is?

*I do not believe you are talking about my home that I live in
right now.*

No, WE are not talking about the physical home you live in.
WE are talking about your home within you, your heart center; your
home that cradles your spirit, full of love and transparency; your
home within that has been there since the beginning of your soul's
birth. This is a place that is only felt, not seen. This is a place where
everything melts, where love's presence is all-encompassing. Your
soul longs to be here. Your soul is one with all that is love. This is
your true home. You no longer will require or need to experience
any separation.

How do we mortal souls get there?

In body, you cannot. In spirit, you can. You can go within and
feel the presence of this home you so long for. You do not have to
die in body to do this either. You can ask to be there, in meditations,
in feelings, in senses. Your heart senses this place and can feel your
way into it. You all have had moments of this place through some
of the things you have done. Your happiest moments have taken you
there. Holding a baby and connecting to the soul of that child have
taken you there even if only for seconds.

When you open to the Oneness of who you are—which is
talked about in the chapter before and in Principle One—the final
step is returning home. When you are looking out to sea, and feel

one with it, and you are inspired to breathe beyond yourself, you are really more than yourself. As you look past the trees in the forest for direction and see the sun seeping through with rays of light, those moments when you can feel love for the flowers and everyone around you and can express appreciation and understand how all share the same frequencies, that is when you have come home.

The reason WE are saying "return home" is because you have been here many times. Like a revolving door, you come back from time to time to remember again who you are and what you are part of. The door is always open for you to return. So many of you may think, *Well, I have to die and go to Heaven for that to happen.* That is what Tammy thought too, when she was given the chapter titles. That is not true and never will be. Your heart will take you there. Your moments of loving someone else will take you there too. Those who are not afraid to love themselves, or another, know well what those moments are. You crave to recreate them over and over again. What you love deeply and connect to is taking you home.

Your heart always remembers, along with your thoughts. Your soul remembers all too well what it feels like to be home. All of your lessons learned are just pebbles in the road you will see or remove so that your walk is easy, or not. Your lessons are reminders of how you have forgotten that love within. Every person, place, or thing is assisting you in remembering what you have forgotten for so long.

All of those incredible souls have raised their soul hands, joining in with you to remember who they are as well, so they can return to the homes within their beings once again. Returning home is essential to all of you. That is why many of you question all that is happening on your planet right now. It is foreign to what your souls know about what your home within is like.

I know Tammy feels like you are all in boot camp or in a universal school of some sort, but in reality, you are hiding from the Light within. You are trapped into believing what is not true of your existence. You believe in what is not real, while the truth is just begging to shine through at your request.

Feel your heart again. Feel your love again. Feel your spirit again. Feel you again in ways of wonder. Feel the joy of living. Feel the joy of knowing what is temporary. Feel the joy of having the opportunity to be home again.

You all have agreed to be embodied to regain your Light of hope and unity. Do not dwell on what it looks like now. Dwell on what you would like to experience and do not settle for crumbs. Settle for home and a return of the Divine Light of all-knowing and all-being. Love cures and defuses all illusions and fears. You are like a huge lighter that just needs to be re-lit and turned up fully. Recognize your Light, and know that that is how you can see others.

As you are home, no fear is present, no stories have any power over you. Being home is absolute stillness. When you are home within, all is healed, and many levels of discomfort are released simultaneously. Do you want to be home again? Do you want to feel and breathe the presence of your Light, your holiness?

Yes I do, and I know the readers would like that too.

Being home is part of you and can never leave you, no matter what you do, say, think, believe or turn away from. You cannot change your home base. Your home is complete love and embracing you back to your Higher Self. Isn't it wonderful to know you cannot screw up where you come from and what you are made of?

Yes it is.

Creating moments of joy and love takes you home as well as anyone who is next to you. WE know WE talk a lot about how your energy affects yourself and others. The important message is that everything you think, feel, and do does affect everyone around you and everyone not around you.

How can you find it inside of you to reach past what is showing up in your play so that you can hold the Light stronger and with joy? Can you just ask to see and feel past what is playing out in your life right now?

Yes, we can do that.

Yes, you can.

You all know all experiences are so temporary. Let go of the troubles and feel the knowingness of God that your Light will prosper and be happy.

Being One again is being One again over and over until there are no more moments of One again, but a sequential flow of Oneness playing over and over again without a beginning or an end to it. That is what is possible in all of you. As certain as WE are about your make-up, as well as your internal make-up, WE are certain you will be home again, not just in moments in your life, but in sequential moments.

How joyful is that? How can you not celebrate the life you are living? Your home is our home. WE all live in that place. Words cannot describe the experience and the connection of Source flowing through you. The words limit what home is. The simplest of words can be like a man, woman, or child who has not had water to drink for days and is given the purest of water to drink. The immediate result of that is the solution and freedom from all fear and the fulfillment of life running through your body, mind, and spirit.

Coming home is experiencing past the array of Oneness. It is love expressed in every soul at the cellular level. Your heart is fully open past even you. Your heart is open to those near you. As you come home, you take them home too. Their hearts are open and expanded because of the love pouring out from you.

Home is where the heart is, as you all say. That is true. Your heart is your home. Your heart does not just beat; your heart is your door to God's glory. Your heart is the opening to the portals to feeling and breathing love.

If you had not ever felt love, you would be gone from your bodies. Why do you think that before people decide to die, they separate from those they love? It is because their heart center is closing. Yes, you may be with them physically, however, they tend to separate for their transitions. Once they have crossed over, their heart is opened again. WE are not saying all souls separate. Some have separated long before their bodies expire. You always have free will from the beginning of your incarnation until your graduation through death. You also have free will to be open to returning home to All That Is at any time—morning, noon or night.

Your free will can deliver you from hell or open the gateways of peace for all of you at any time in your life cycles. What would you rather be doing? You agreed to be incarnated, so how are you going to choose? The love that can deliver you from all stories and illusions is available in every instant. Your customs are not of God. What is of God is your love and only that.

As in the tag line, you will be past the separation and into the Oneness, and then like a pop, your heart will open and overflow your being with love unknown to most. Once this happens, in intervals your world will seem meaningless, and the reality of who you are shimmers through. The only thing of importance is each other, not the ego part of you that says what size your body is or any of the many other repetitive thoughts that are irrelevant.

The smallness of your ego is flushed away. How many times have you witnessed someone or yourself as one with everything to the point of feeling that love expand from your heart chakra?

I have, but not so many times. What will happen if this occurs more frequently?

What will happen is that your world will be anew. Your crisis will disappear in seconds, minutes, days. You will shatter the worldly effects of fear into oblivion. You will create a world that is loving and serving each other. You will eliminate all lack, judgment, and darkness.

You will open portals that match the frequencies of your new ways. You may diminish the possibility of even needing a world as you know it. The options are unlimited.

Why hold yourself back to only what imaginary boxes can create? On the outside, if WE must use that term, your boxes are so small and your plays are extremely repetitious. Leaving the illusions can only create home for all of you. WE have said this many times, but going home is going within you, to see your heart opening up, to feel your days, to open your heart to others with compassion and trust and hope in yourself and everyone.

Sounds so easy in words.

It is easy, but your stories hold you back. What is ironic is those in pain are those who have closed their hearts off from themselves. The souls on your planet who have their hearts open are living deeper, more meaningful lives. You were never meant to be alone or to hide or close your doors to others. You were made to share, to brew love frequencies all over your planet in all ways.

Oneness is knowing and believing you are not separate and being home is feeling you are not separate. Feeling two hearts or more that are joining is like a kaleidoscope of souls morphing past bodies and into dimensions of everything that is. You are shifting in motion in a timeless and incredible Light that is beyond your conception. Your mind is limited to your beingness, and your heart is unlimited to what is. As you connect your minds and your hearts, all worlds disappear as your new world appears beyond your physical eyes.

Being home has always been your soul's desire. In spite of your worldly routines and fears, you can open that door within your heart to vibrate into returning home. Your awareness to choose to co-create an opening for God to expand within you, is how you are home again.

I love this, William.

You should. You have written today when you were not in the best of places emotionally. How do you feel now?

I feel better, and I am open to expanding my heart so I can experience home again.

Wonderful. How about all of you reading this? Are you willing to expand your heart so you can connect to your home again?

WE are here to deliver you all from your cycles of madness. You are us and WE are you. WE deliver you and you deliver us. That is how it is and how it has always been.

You are brave souls to have incarnated at this time, and WE want to say how proud and honored WE are to be here to help you all. Your opening to your heart center and your mind excites all the universes and the galaxies in existence as well as those not in existence.

Your motivation can come from the child you have not had yet in your next lifetime or maybe the child or children you are raising right now. Your motivation can come from deciding you have had enough pain and that you are ready to learn from love and joy. To be glad is to be happy with what is, to be glad the cycles of pain are over, and to know your home is a part of you. What a celebration of life you are!

I am William, and WE see YOU as us, blending into Oneness and our hearts' centers are now connecting to you. You are the masters. WE look to you and have always looked to you. WE now see each other as One and thriving. As your heart is opening up to the connection to us, you are opening up to those around you. You are not afraid to live again, to hold another, to love another, and to love the communities around you—to love the cities and the states and the countries. You are now open to loving your planet Earth and past your Earth to the Heavens. You are now open to your guides, your angels, your God. WE know your souls as complete jewels of Heaven.

God is living and experiencing with you, in you, and around you constantly. What is there not to love? Your hearts are beacons. WE can see your flickers of light from the Heavens. Why are you not willing to open your Light sources? WE are watching your heart as it beats, but WE wait patiently for you to open your heart's center fully. You are the beacons of Light that can light the universes with your hearts and your essence.

Live fully. WE drink the waters with you as you drink. Your drink is our drink. Your movements and your thoughts are our thoughts as well. WE blend into your being as you blend into us. Let us all come together to see each other as saviors and as fellow Light beings. Our love can change everything. Are you ready for a new play? The director is open for new scripts all the time.

WE want to thank you all for reading this book, and may you be inspired and open-hearted to changing your soul's destiny. With all love and Light, you matter. You are all universes and time zones of life—past, present and future. WE hold the vision that all of you will muster the creations within yourselves to live a life free of pain; that your souls and hearts will join like weaves of thread with each other until there is only a reflection of Light over all of your planet where you cannot see the threads anymore, just Light because you chose love instead.

Be brave souls. Be the ones that move your planet into the God Light it is, where you will no longer need your world of pain, but live in one of beauty and a vastness of utmost love. Feel the love within your hearts and allow the Holy Spirit to fill you up with that unseen love that you so desire and need to live.

Ask to wear the unseen etheric jacket of God's glory around you and everyone else on your planet, like a huge golden blanket that covers your whole planet. Ask to wear God's presence. Ask to walk in God's shoes. Ask to see in God's Light. Ask to hear in God's voice to speak a new way. Ask to touch everything as a God would, owning the God within you.

Since WE all know and believe that you are God, WE are not worried or scared, because as you, the Gods of Light will shatter the ego completely. You will have no value in it anymore. The God Source energy that you are, will deliver you to the complete remembrance that WE are One, once again for the last time.

Alas, my dear loved ones, WE salute you as our sisters and brothers and as our savior. Carry on with vigor and let the Light force within you carry you throughout the Heavens and the universes of your time. May WE continue to cross each other's paths as WE heal, and deliver us all into complete Oneness, never to return to any delusional dimension that even thinks for a second that WE need to be separate in any way. Call it a dream or a reality, it does not matter. What matters is that WE are all One again, without the imaginary egos or plots.

With all our love and Divine Order to you and yours, let's create harmony together for the last time on your planet and undo any beliefs in separation.

Join in our frequencies so WE can stand above all battlefields in all lifetimes to Heavens you have not experienced as of yet. Believe in home again—that home within you that knows. With all of our unconditional love, WE hold you dearly, not leaving you, but assisting you. Call on us, our lines are always open.

Amen to you all. You are never alone. Can you really do this? Can you live and thrive on your planet? Yes, you can. You now have the principles that can deliver you in every second of the day. Go live and co-create with these twelve principles.

WE salute you and bow to your bravery and your love for truth. I am William, your beloved brother and spiritual guide. WE see you lifted and healed and in Heaven as you come home once and for all. No longer needing any illusion to experience, only the love is expressed through all of you. Embrace fully your God Selves and allow your hearts to sing songs of celebration, as WE are joined as ONE, forever more.

Remembering One, Once Again

Afterword

Before I close, I'd like to leave you with a few final words from me personally. It took writing this book with William to truly understand my own value and release my false beliefs as to what would make me happy. In spite of my work, which has given me more life and value, I could not own joy for myself until I was honest and willing to change my thoughts and feelings about me.

What I have learned for sure, is that we can discover our inner truth without being stuck in Principle One, and that the only thing that matters is our connection with each other. Always remember to be kind, and to be grateful for what and who is showing up in your play. It is so easy to look at what is not working. Laugh more often and try not to take life so seriously. Know that forgiveness is not just a word but an act of loving yourself and a gift for others to witness.

Take the time to savor moments that feed you, and embrace the beautiful souls you all are. Those are precious gifts that not only confirm your beauty but also align your greatness to be present with you.

I can honestly say that when you have gone through hardships, in any form, that bring you to your knees, they are a blessing because you will rise up stronger, deeper, and more loyal to all of your relationships, especially with yourself. The small petty thoughts do not matter and you are alive with a thirst for truth within your being that shows up differently. I have come to appreciate everyone that has come into my play—both in the past and the present—with such love and awe. I now enjoy the differences in everyone and know there are no accidents in who has come into my life. Take time everyday to be compassionate, loving, and loyal, knowing everyone is doing their best to show up, and that if someone is in fear (like the *Course in Miracles* says), that it is a cry for love, and to not take it personally.

I have made a promise to myself to not judge as much, to see the beauty in everyone I meet, and to let go of the past because you cannot change it. I give such reverence to our journeys together. I thank God for bringing in so many kind, wonderful souls who have touched my heart—from my family and friends, to all of the wonderful clients who have come into my life and taught me what love is.

When William gave me the vision for the book cover and the six levels, he showed me how these levels interact with each other. William showed me that there were white streams of light showing up in all of the six levels, giving each level a life of its own. I asked William what the streams of white lights were. William said, in the most loving voice, "That is The WE—the God Selves in your beings—that are sending waves of light to help you, to pull you out of your darkness and fears." I can tell you that I cried with such appreciation and a knowing that we are never alone. As William said, it will take twenty-two percent at level four to change the planet. As we change ourselves to a higher frequency past the fourth level, we will all rise into our oneness once and for all. Are you with me? I know you are. I know we are here together to shine bright—past our fears and our smallness. Let's all shine brightly so that we can surpass level four in the book. Let's do this together—knowing we are all in this together. I love you all.

A million hugs and a million smiles,

Tammy J. Holmes

WITH GRATITUDE AND LOVE

This is my chocolate and the salt in my popcorn—to express my gratitude for those who have helped me in some way or another as this book came to be.

First, I would like to thank Jane Landers for all of the hours she has spent with me in editing and believing in the book as much as I have. This book would not have happened without her in my life. Your input and your heart are on all of the pages.

To my family, my son James Thrower, my sister Diana and her husband Don and to my mother Amelia—thank you for your love and support. To Jane's mother who is my mamma number two, Mary Saalman, thank you for treating me like your own daughter.

To those angels who helped edit the book: Heather Clarke you rock and I love you—you are such a light for the Phoenix area—I do see your center showing up. To Tessa Herrington, for your honesty and your friendship, thank you. To Jan Whalen for your valuable knowledge and helping me connect to the right people to finish the book.

To Don Enevoldsen for formatting the book and your expertise. Artwork. Ann Rothan for the front page and the six levels in chapter one. Thanks to Crystal McMahon for doing the book cover layout.

To some of my friends who stood by me—Audrey Roybal, Gail Wiggs, Sandy Johnston, Dr. Maria Esvel Yannguas, Della Hale, Debbie Nicholas—thank you for supporting me throughout this book.

To Chris Holbert for creating the web site and telling me in 2008 after a workshop that the principles need to be in a book to share with others.

To Joanne Tedesco, Sandy Rogers, Vickie Champion, Dehbra Taylor for your relentless dedication to believe in your dreams and for being there for me. To Terri Bowersock, Jacque Ardebili, Jeorgetta Douglas-Acosta—your unconditional love and your lights have touched my soul on a very deep level.

To the twelve ladies in our Circle of Light group where we support each other and talk every two weeks about our lives and hold each other accountable.

To my Phoenix base friends from the time I moved here in 2004 to the present. You all have inspired me to be the best I can be. To my California friends from Bakersfield who are family to me—boy, do I have memories of our past to laugh about!

To all of my Los Angeles friends: I love you all; you were my heros for allowing me to read for you in the beginning, in 96, and teach classes out of Audrey's house.

To all of the wonderful souls I met in Texas in 2009, you are inspiring and your dedication to your life journeys blows me away.

To all of the metaphysical shops, healers, and readers who are brave enough to jump without nets to support everyone's growth.

For the Course In Miracles for changing my thoughts and for feeding my soul on a daily basis.

I would like express my deepest thanks for the clients who I have worked with over the years. All of the clients from America, to the United Kingdom, to Canada, and everywhere else continue to confirm that there are many realms in existence.

To William for believing in this book, never leaving me, and always showing up. Your guidance is deeply valued and appreciated.

For the song Velvet Rope by Janet Jackson. William loved the words, and so I played this song more than a 1000 times as William and I wrote this book.

To all of my past, present and future guides who have shown up to teach me, even when I protested.

To Oprah, I love your new network, OWN. Your courage to stay true to teaching what is truth is inspiring and educational. May God continue to bless you. Thank you. When you know better, you do better.

Remembering One, Once Again

ABOUT THE AUTHOR

Tammy J Holmes is the founder and CEO of Mind Your Intentions. Tammy brings universal hope through spiritual coaching, mediumship, and her talks and group readings.

Tammy gathers and connects those who are ready to see their life through new eyes. With a data base of 50,000 she connects her nationwide and international clientele with their higher purpose through, books, CD's, and Personalized spiritual coaching. Tammy has coached and read over 30,000 clients since 1996. In 2006 People magazine reported her story of physically locating the body of Terri Bowersock's mother in the desert.

To create transformation on a grander scale, she produced over 25 of The Awakening Conferences, thus connecting other internationally renowned speakers such as Marianne Williamson, Michael and Rickie Beckwich, and Don Miguel Ruiz with thousands seeking spiritual growth.

*Website: **www.TammyjHolmes.com***

Remembering One, Once Again

NOTES

Remembering One, Once Again

CPSIA information can be obtained at www.ICGtesting.com
Printed in the USA
BVOW071703010513

319622BV00002B/2/P